Rapid Crisis Resolution

Rapid Crisis Resolution

CHARLES CRESSON WOOD

Disclaimers

This book is intended to provide helpful guidance and perspective for those facing difficult personal problems and/or crises. While the material in this book has been prepared by a trained psycho-spiritual counselor (Pathwork Helper™), it does not replace or eliminate, nor is it intended to replace or eliminate, the need for the services of a medical doctor, psychologist, psychotherapist, psychiatrist, or other helping professionals. Individuals in need of those services are strongly urged to consult with such professionals. In this book, no medical advice is given, and no promises are made, regarding the diagnosis or cure of any conditions.

The personal story section found in each chapter of this book makes reference to a fictional individual who is a composite of several people. Use of such fictional people is a literary device intended solely to illustrate the primary point of the chapter. The words employed to describe these fictional people are not intended to describe, or in any way apply to, any particular individual, whether living or dead. Any similarity to a particular individual is purely coincidental, and is not intended by the author.

Copyright Notices

**Another Relevant Book by
Charles Cresson Wood**

Opening to Abundance: A 31-Day Process of Self-Discovery
Publisher: Pathwork Press (2004)
ISBN-10: 0961477792
ISBN-13: 978-0961477790

http://www.pathwork.org

Dedication

To Eva Broch Pierrakos,
for her beautiful dance through life,
which included the Pathwork lectures

"It is not the strongest of the species that survives, nor the most intelligent, but the most responsive to change."
– Charles Darwin, 1809

"As a single footstep will not make a path on the earth, so a single thought will not make a pathway in the mind. To make a deep physical path, we walk again and again. To make a deep mental path, we must think over and over the kind of thoughts we wish to dominate our lives."
– Henry David Thoreau, 1854

"No one is given more to bear than he or she is able to [handle]. And every hardship is but the effect of a cause that was created by the self and, therefore has to be solved and gone through by the self."
– Eva Broch Pierrakos, 1956

Table of Contents

Acknowledgements

THIS BOOK IS based on the Pathwork, a psychological, emotional, and spiritual process defined in the Pathwork lectures. The Pathwork lectures—over several thousand pages in total— were compiled by the late Eva Broch Pierrakos, and they are available to everyone at both http://www.pathworklectures.com/ and http://www.pathwork.org/ (the unedited version is recommended). Readers of these profound lectures need not provide any personal data, answer any survey, or jump over any procedural hurdle in order to access the lectures online. All the lectures are available for free. Those who have benefitted from the process described in this book, those who want to take the depth of their personal process to the next level, will definitely want to read these lectures.

The Pathwork process is supportive of those who adhere to all religious faiths and all spiritual practices. It is also suitable for those who do not identify with a particular religious faith, and/ or do not currently follow a spiritual practice. The Pathwork process is inclusive in nature; it emphasizes living in truth, taking self-responsibility for one's life, and understanding the many aspects of one's own consciousness.

The author gratefully acknowledges the amazing gift given to the world by Eva Broch Pierrakos and those who worked with her. In writing this book, the author wishes to help disseminate this information more widely and to give back in acknowledgement of all that he has personally received thereby.

This author has worked intensely with the Pathwork material for over twenty-five years. He is a trained Pathwork helper (counselor), and he has written another Pathwork book entitled *Opening To Abundance: A 31-Day Process Of Self-Discovery* (available via http://www.amazon.com/). Nonetheless, for the author there is much personal work still to be done.

Rather than being discouraging, this last paragraph's personal history data point is offered as an indication of the richness of, and vast array of transcendent truths contained in the lectures. The process defined by the Pathwork is a multi-lifetime endeavor in which people evolve on all levels, gradually becoming liberated from both misconceptions and untruths.

This book is intended to help readers become more flexible and open to change, more positively intentioned, and genuinely committed to evolving themselves. It is additionally intended to help readers resolve a particularly difficult problem, such as a crisis. In the process of achieving these goals, the author hopes that readers will also discover a new and more empowered way to live, as well as obtain a sense for what life is asking of them now.

Although this self-help book has been written for use in a private journal, beyond the first few months of personal work, nobody will be able to successfully do this work alone. This is because we all have blind spots, resistant places, places where we unreasonably defend, misconceptions, erroneous images about the nature of life, and other issues which cause us to see life in ways that aren't accurate. At least one other person is needed to provide a grounding point, a mirror, and a coach to urge the reader to take the next step forward. Generally, that person is a Pathwork helper (a trained Pathwork counselor), but it could in some situations be a teacher, or even another seeker of the deeper truth.

The author gratefully acknowledges the influence of the Pathwork helpers and teachers with whom he has worked. Particular thanks are extended to Barbara Azzara, Brian O'Donnell, Susan and Donovan Thesenga, Keith Covington, Gene Humphrey, and Alison Green-Barton. He additionally gratefully notes the contributions and assistance provided by co-truth-seekers Sheila James, Bonnie Chung, Matt Fluty, Christine Portney, Taitha Killion, Gregory Alper, Lea Itkin, Barbara Stannard, John Backus, John Shordike, Judith Saly, Gustavo Damasio Monteiro, Kelly McDowell Moeller, Dimitri and Catherine Karas, Andi Kiva, and Deborah Holmes. Appreciative thanks are sent to Natalie Mortensen for her editing assistance and Jennifer Kenyon for her iris flower drawing. Finally, special and emphatic thanks go out to my girlfriend and spiritual partner, Peggy Hilden.

Introduction

IF YOU HAVE a serious or difficult problem, perhaps a crisis, and you know something has to change in order to resolve it, this is the book for you. If you want to quit smoking, find a new job, find a compatible mate, stick with your diet to lose a lot of weight, go back to school to get a degree, this book will help you discover a unity of intention to proceed in the direction that you consciously articulate. If you have recently declared bankruptcy, been fired from your job, or left behind by a spouse, this book will help you to gather yourself together so as to constructively go on to create a new life. Whatever your serious problem or crisis, this book will help you discover the place within you that is genuinely committed to a positive change, so that you can then follow through with the change you consciously desire.

The book is intended to bring to the surface all those unconscious and unexpressed parts of your psyche that say "no"—all those parts which are in opposition to your consciously articulated intention. Once out in the open, these nay-saying parts can be examined, compared with reality, and directly challenged. In many cases, these inner parts will be easily dealt with because they are based on misconceptions, misinterpretations, maladjustments to historical events, and other unrealistic thought patterns. In other cases, further investigation will be required to reveal a still deeper level of resistance, opposition, objection, negation, and the like.

How the physical world manifests for each of us is a result of our own personal inner world, the combination of all the layers of consciousness in our psyche. Psychologists now partially recognize this phenomenon with the phrase "self-fulfilling prophesy." But there is much more to it, as is explained further in this book. The broader and more encompassing view of self-responsibility found in this book is very good news, because it means that we each have way more power to change our lives for the better than we have previously believed.

Although few of us actually use the ability, we can deliberately evolve our own consciousness. We have much more power over our thoughts and feelings that we generally believe. This book is intended to assist you the reader in your efforts to change your beliefs, attitudes, thoughts, and feelings. When you achieve positive success with this important inner work, then your outer experience inevitably changes as well. When you shift your inner world, you will naturally undertake changes in the outer world that you previously found inconceivable.

In the majority of things that we do, we humans are motivated by a mix of lower-self (negative) intentions as well as higher-self (positive) intentions. This mix, and the resulting conflict of intentions, creates unpredictable, and often unwanted, results out there in the world. Unless they have done a significant amount of inner work, most people suffer through a life made up of many mysterious and inexplicable experiences. Unless they have undertaken a deep process of self-exploration and transformation, such as the one introduced in this book, they never understand why the results of their efforts disappointingly fall short of those results they consciously desire. This book can thus help to illuminate the deeper reasons why you may have been frustrated in the achievement of an important goal, and that illumination can then prove instrumental in generating your expanded ability to manifest the goal you desire.

This multi-dimensional and often-conflicting nature of human consciousness explains why an apparently positive action may have a disastrous outcome. The undesirable result may be caused by a negative intention that has been heretofore unacknowledged. For example, an expensive present bought for another might offend the recipient, who may think that she is being manipulated. Likewise, an apparently negative event may turn out to be a blessing in disguise. This could happen if the negative event vividly reveals one's needed inner work. For example, a person could contract a serious sickness to create the personal space that allows them to take time for themselves, so that they can compassionately deal with the unresolved emotions that they have kept bottled up inside. Behind this externally negative situation (the sickness) was a positive intention to advance the individual's personal evolution. So, both clarifying and aligning your intentions are essential keys to creating the results you desire. This book will help you unify these intentions and allow them to become consistent and harmonious, so that the desired change you seek will naturally follow.

This is not an entertainment book. It is instead a roll-up-your-sleeves and get-down-to-work practical self-help book. To discover its real value, you must, with serious intent, honestly answer the questions at the end of each chapter before proceeding to the next chapter. To answer these questions in writing, at least fifteen minutes are strongly recommended for each chapter.

Let's pause to reflect on your inner process for just a moment. When you just read about the time required (in the prior paragraph, in case you deliberately ignored it), how did your lower self react? Perhaps it said something like: "What? No way! I'm not going to do that!" Alternatively, perhaps the lower self said something like: "Doesn't the author know I've got a lot of important things to do!!!?" You are invited to check-in with yourself, and listen to what your lower self just said. In so many of us, it is this and related places inside of us that says "no." That "no" in turn seriously gets in our way, prevents us from manifesting the change, the inner growth, the crisis resolution, the inner peace, and the happiness that we desire.

By answering the exercise questions you will be taking the time to notice what's going on inside of you -- time that you probably have not devoted to self-examination in the days gone past. By answering the exercise questions you put yourself in a place of choice between the old-way of doing things and the new-way of doing things. If you don't see that there is a choice, because you didn't take the time to look inside yourself, it will be very difficult for you to resolve your crisis in a desirable way.

If you genuinely want to change your life for the better, you will be required to do some serious work. This Pathwork process, although very powerful and very time-efficient, is not magic. This is the real world, and if you want results, this inner work will take dedicated effort. As the bodybuilders put it: "No pain, no gain." So the author invites you to commit yourself to manifesting the results you consciously seek, and paying the price to get those results as well.

Before you start reading this book, the author strongly suggests that you purchase or otherwise obtain a blank journal book without lines, with lots of empty pages, waiting for your writings, pictures, visions, and scribbles. While it is possible to answer the questions at the end of each chapter with a computer, instead the author recommends handwritten answers, hand-rendered drawings, sketched pictures and tables, etc., that are rendered via the use of a pen or pencil on paper. This is because the hand rendering is more personal, and it helps to access a deeper and more creative, and less business-like, part of your consciousness.

You will also need a place where you can safely store this journal, a hidden spot where it will not be discovered and read by anyone prying into your personal affairs. This last requirement is important, because if you don't have good strong boundaries involving privacy and confidentiality, then you won't be able to relax and honestly respond to the personal questions posed at the end of each chapter.

When answering each chapter's questions in writing, to get the maximum value out of this book you will need to be brutally honest about both your life and your inner world. You will need to put all this down in your journal, and feel confident that this information will not be revealed to unauthorized parties, until you (and only you) are ready and willing to disclose it.

Answering the questions with your thoughts alone, or with words spoken out loud, will in no way have the same positive impact as writing all this down. Writing focuses the mind in a way that thinking alone, or thinking and speaking combined, does not. Writing integrates multiple levels of your consciousness. Writing demarcates boundaries, and makes things clear in black-and-white terms. Writing also gives you something to review, to challenge, and to later embellish. Thoughts alone, or thoughts accompanied by spoken words, can do only so much. Writing your answers will give you the support to remember those aspects of your unevolved psyche that have a direct bearing on the changes that you say you want to bring about. If only thoughts, or only thoughts with spoken words, are used to answer these questions, your lower self will deliberately forget what just transpired (and thereby deviously justify not changing because the reasons supporting a change seem to have mysteriously dissolved). Having these answers in clear and definitive writings also helps to eliminate the lower-self justification not to take action because one doesn't know what's happening, and because one is confused as to why things are the way they are.

The author is not intent on convincing you to adopt and/or maintain any particular beliefs. Nor is he intent on enrolling you into any particular worldview, or having you become part of any religious or spiritual group. The Pathwork, which is discussed further in the Acknowledgements section, does not have a creed or dogma. There is no initiation process through which the author wishes to take you. Consistent with that same philosophy, of simply wishing to assist other people with their personal journeys through life, please don't believe anything that you read in this book just because it appears herein. Believe it instead because you actually tested it in your life, and can therefore speak from personal knowledge and experience, and accordingly you know that it works for you.

If you aren't ready to receive an idea found in this book, you won't understand it. Each of us has a point in time when we're ready to hear certain things. If you aren't there yet, that's normal, and nothing to worry about. Rereading the words a few times is recommended, and often that's what's needed when we reach such a point, especially if we are resistant to receiving a new idea. But if you're still left scratching your head, and you just can't seem to get it, simply move on to the next idea. On the other hand, if you do understand a new idea, please don't simply accept it. Instead, mull it over, and entertain how you might live your life differently if that idea was in fact true and also part of your way of navigating the waters of life. If the new idea still sounds intriguing, if it sounds as though it might be the seed for a new way to be, go on and try it out in your life, and see if it creates desirable results. If it works for you, then perhaps there is some truth to it.

To get the most out of this book, the author also recommends that the reader say a prayer before undertaking every chapter's written journal exercises. This is optional, but if you do it, such a prayer will supercharge your results. Depending on the relationship that you have with God (Goddess, G-d, Allah, Elohim, Creator, Almighty, Absolute Being, Infinite Spirit, Holy Spirit, Higher Power, All-That-Is, Great Mystery, whatever name you want to use), then you might say a prayer such as:

"Help me, please God, help me to understand why my life is as it is now. I ask for inspiration, courage, tenacity, and strength to do the work of aligning my consciousness with your will and your spiritual laws. I will do the work, but please reveal to me what that work entails."

If you are having an allergic reaction to the word "God," then please remember that the author is not talking about the

God of organized religion, or the God you were taught about in school. Instead, think of your own personal experience of God. Your own connection with God may, for example, be found in meditation, or when you are immersed in wild nature, in times of intense and sustained exercise, or perhaps in times of blissful forgetfulness about yourself. Think of a higher intelligence, a superior wisdom that created this universe. This definition is not limited, restricted, or circumscribed. Don't limit God and how He/She/It can work with you. What you call God is not really important; what is important is that you don't let this reference word become a stumbling block to opening up your connection with God, to expanding your personal development process so that you work more intimately with God. You need to have a name for God in order to ask for God's help; you need to have a name for God in order to think clearly about your relationship to God. To evolve yourself rapidly, to make the big changes you want to make, you will need God's help. So, if you can, regard the word "God" as used in this book as a placeholder. It is simply the most convenient and most widely employed word pointing in the direction of this great intelligence.

Returning to the above prayer, there's nothing special about the particular words used above. You are invited to make up your own words, and change them regularly, in response to both your personal needs and your life's circumstances. Have your prayer be dynamic and inspired by the nature of the work you're doing in the moment. For example, if you don't believe in God, you could simply affirm your intention to be in truth and bring your best to life. Likewise, if you are uncomfortable using the word "God" or similar words, then use other words like Life, Love, Truth, Nature, or the Light. There are many possibilities.

Whatever your prayer, attunement, or affirmation may be, you should engage with this book as though it is more than simply an intellectual exercise. This book works on many levels. To get the most out of it, you will need to engage your heart, your feelings, your will, your soul, and other aspects of your psyche. While specific instructions will follow later in the book, at this point you are invited to intuitively feel into what it would be like to open up on multiple levels.

Although this book provides an "introduction" to the Pathwork, the matters that it deals with are far from simple and inconsequential. Many feelings and emotions, as well as new thought experiments, will be stirred up by your inner work, and that is as the author intended. Savor the book and take your time with it. Ideally, you would read and answer the questions at the rate of one chapter a day. Be aware of how your lower self wants you to rush through the book, wants to gloss over things that might be uncomfortable to look at, wants you to get it over with as soon as possible. Also allow yourself to create the time and space so that you can provide an extended answer to a question, if that's what you feel is appropriate. If you need to, go back over a chapter until you feel ready to move on. Only you know the proper pace to go through this material. Similarly, if you want more information about a specific set of ideas in a particular chapter, then go to Appendix A and identify and read the relevant Pathwork lecture (they are available on the Internet for free, as discussed in the Acknowledgements section). Give the book some time to work on you, and give yourself some time to settle into the multi-dimensional work to be done.

Many people who read another Pathwork book written by the author, also found it valuable to reread the author's other Pathwork book a year or two after first working with it. The book you are reading now will probably likewise be useful if reviewed years later. Over that intervening period, both your circumstances and your state of consciousness are likely to have changed markedly, so your answers to the chapter questions will most likely also be significantly different. During this intervening period, if you have continued your process of personal transformation, you will also be likely to notice: how your range of possible emotional responses to life has widened, how you have become aware of many more action-oriented options than were previously acknowledged, how you are so much more in touch with your true intentions, how much more quickly you change when life asks that of you, and how rapidly so many aspects of your life in general have been changing for the better.

Once you get involved with the Pathwork process, if you are diligent and sincere in your endeavors, you will see amazing results. To track your progress over a long period of time can be an exciting and illuminating process. Accordingly, you may wish to hold onto your journal, so that you are able to make the above-mentioned before-and-after comparison based on your prior written answers.

Enjoy and God bless!

Charles Cresson Wood
Pathwork Helper
Mendocino, California
http://www.abundantreality.com/
March 2017

1

Asking to Know the
Whole Truth

Affirmation:

O N SOME LEVEL, I know how to bring about the change I seek. I want to know all of the truth about myself, and I will not cringe or look away in vanity, cowardice, or self-pity. I ask for Divine* help here—may I be supported in seeing and receiving all of this truth.

Core Idea:

We all have powers, faculties, talents and gifts that we aren't using. Part of us doesn't want to know about them, or how they might help us bring about the change that we seek. Part of us doesn't want to know who we really are. This resisting part wants us to remain

---

* If you have not already read the Introduction—where the limitless and unrestricted definition of the Divine is covered—the author strongly urges you to do so soon.

both in the dark and in denial. This part must be recognized and overcome before we can proceed with the big change that we seek.

There are many things that we don't understand about life, about the world, about the nature of consciousness, and about why we are here. As a thought experiment, consider this: part of the reason we are here is to grow spiritually, to learn about ourselves, and to learn about the nature of life (or God, if you will). The school of life takes a unique form for each of us because the curriculum is uniquely tailored to our individual needs. On a deeper level, we all know what the curriculum is for our own lives. If we honestly ask for guidance here, and if we have some patience and genuine openness, we will be shown what we need to learn, and what we need to change.

But we cannot access this place of a deeper knowing, we cannot receive this guidance, if there is part of us which does not wish to know ourselves, our life path, what needs our attention, and what needs to change. This resisting place that wants to be in denial is threatened by the truth. It already knows that if it were to be aligned with the truth, if what was really going on was out in the open, then changes would be made soon thereafter. It is this place of resistance that must be brought into the light for examination, must be brought into the light for healing.

We must honestly ask ourselves whether we are ready for the full truth, the all-encompassing objective truth. Perhaps we'd be embarrassed if a certain truth were to come forward. Perhaps we couldn't deal with the fact that we haven't yet overcome a certain childish fault. Maybe we couldn't bear the thought that we have not yet handled a certain problem that we believed we "put to bed" long ago. Or perhaps we have built a life on an assumption about who we thought we were, and we don't want to have to tear down that false structure.

Contrary to what this resisting part believes, there is much happiness in the frank, open, and straight admission of the truth. We don't need to tell anybody about this truth, if we don't wish to do so. But with ourselves, and with God—there must be honesty if we are going to change. It is only with the stability and security of the truth that the power to make a big change can come. In our humility, in our commitment to know the absolute grounded truth about ourselves, are the seeds of a new and more evolved self.

As long as we have closed the door to the truth about who we are, and what in us needs to change, our life will continue to be characterized by the pain and suffering that we have experienced up to this moment. But if we can have the courage to honestly embrace all of the truth, if we can in humility and modesty accept that truth, then we have a new inner climate in which a lasting change can take place.

We need to ask God for help here; we need to ask to be shown the truth about our situation. At the same time, we must not demand that this truth show up in a certain way.

We must patiently allow God's spirit helpers to communicate it to us in their own way, a way suitable for our own school of life. The answers may come in the form of another person's words, in a glance from a stranger, in a magazine article, or perhaps in an electronic mail message. The answers may be revealed during our meditation, or come from a sudden and unexpected epiphany about our life. The answers may already be there in our lives, for example in a diary, or in a novel we have read.

These answers, whatever they may be, need to be embraced with self-love and acceptance. Although the truth of our situations might be inconvenient and unflattering, the very fact that we've embraced it is cause for celebration. When we embrace our truth, we transcend who we thought we were, the limits we imposed on ourselves, and the fixedness of how the rest of our life was going to look.

It is best if we regard these new truths about the parts that need to evolve as temporary truths. They are only who we are in this moment; they do not define our ultimate and true being. Who we really are—a creation of the Divine—is the part that knows the truth. This latter part recreates itself and has the courage to look at the straight and unvarnished truth. Who we truly are is the part that makes this process possible. Discovering it will open our connection with the Divine, as well as empower us to make the big changes for which we yearn.

Personal Story:

Larry had a great life, or at least that's what people told him. He had good health, his own small business in the fishing industry, a loving and intelligent wife, and a comfortable house in the woods that he built with his own hands. He had a number of good friends, and was recognized as a community leader in his small town. But inside himself, Larry considered himself to be an abysmal failure.

Larry was upset that he was not rich, and by that he meant really "big-time rich." He considered wealth to be the true measure of a man's worth. He thought that if a man was a multimillionaire, then he was somebody of true value, a success. Larry was also upset that he did not have a trophy wife, a spectacularly beautiful woman, a wife who would make other men envious of him. Although he didn't tell his wife about these judgments, on some level he kept belittling himself because he thought he didn't measure up.

In a discussion over dinner with Oliver, a buddy of his, Larry got to talking about what it meant to be a success. He revealed that he felt he could never get the approval and acceptance that he wanted from others. During this discussion, he started to see just how much of his inner life revolved around obtaining this approval and acceptance. What his buddy said next really floored Larry. Oliver told Larry that he had defined his own criteria, and that according to these criteria he was already a success.

Oliver went on to say that he didn't accept what society told him success was all about. He talked about how advertisements wanted people to think that buying stuff made them successful, but that this was just a con job. Oliver recounted how his parents wanted him to be a lawyer or a doctor, and that to them his success was all about elevating their status in the community. He mentioned the details of what he had been taught a man "had to do" in order to be successful, but that too was about others pushing their ideas on him. Oliver rejected all these notions.

Oliver went on to tell Larry, that he, and only he, now defines whether he is a success. His criteria was really quite simple: (1) is he growing as a person; (2) does he have enough money to meet his basic human needs; (3) is he making a genuine contribution to life that employs his unique talents and gifts; and (4) does he have a family, friends, work associates, and a wider community of people around him that is characterized by a loving connection? Oliver said that, at that moment, he had all of those things, and so he was therefore a success.

Larry was challenged by the conversation, and thought about it on and off for a few days thereafter. He came to see how greedy he was for the approval and validation of others, and how he had become beholden to them for his sense of self. He also understood that he could instead attain much the same approval and validation from both God and himself.

The big change, which Larry had not expected, came about in his attitude. He started to see how his harsh self-judgment, how his belief in his not being good enough, or rich enough, or great enough to attract a trophy wife, were making him profoundly unhappy. Larry began to feel really free, inexplicably joyous, and deeply self-responsible for creating his own life. He also started to like himself in a new and different way, a way with which he had no previous experience. Larry's answer came through Oliver, but it was only an answer because he was open to receiving it as such.

Journal Questions:

(1) What part of you does not want to be in the full truth, in the all-encompassing objective truth, about the area in which you hope to bring about a change? Why is this part blocking the truth? Is such a blocking really in your best long-run interest? Explain specifically why or why not.

(2) Suppose you were waiting to cross a street at a busy and dangerous traffic intersection with a stoplight. The intersection has no bell or other devices that could let a blind person know when the light had changed. Then you noticed a blind man with a cane nearby, wanting to cross the street, but acting confused and scared. Wouldn't you naturally, and without resentment or hesitation, offer to help him cross the street safely at the right time? Now

suppose there is a part in you that is blind and scared—a part that has not yet seen the truth surrounding your predicament. With the same humility, compassion, acceptance, patience, and desire to help, can you offer some support to that part? What would you offer so that this part might be helped along the road to seeing the truth?

(3) Separately, consider that you may need to go through a spiritual test of your sincerity before you can receive the whole truth that you need to know, so that the change you desire can then take place. How might your commitment to receiving the absolute truth about yourself be tested? If this test has already happened, or if it is happening right now, did you pass the test? If this test will take place in the future, how would you like to then respond?

2

Resolving to Give Your Very Best

Affirmation:

IN THIS MOMENT, I choose to give my very best. I bring a single-pointed focus to the change I seek to bring about; I give all of myself to this effort. I vow to fight the fight, to do the work, to apply myself with commitment and determination, so as to bring this change about.

Core Idea:

Since they have some basic personal knowledge of the market for real estate, in general people do not expect that a beautiful mansion would be given to them without paying a high price. They understand that a mansion will of course cost considerably more than a shack. There is no argument about these facts of life. Nonetheless, when it comes to spiritual development, many people expect to be able to have an expansive, abundant, meaningful, joyous, and

— 9 —

loving lifestyle without having done the work to achieve these states of being. As is the case with a house, they will have to work for these more evolved spiritual states. More specifically, they will have to fight with, subdue, and later train their lower self (the un-evolved part of their psyche). We can, each of us, resolve right now to do the necessary work to bring about the change we desire; we can resolve to fight this noble fight.

To successfully fight this fight, we must be aware of the tricks used by the lower self to prevent us from even entering into, and staying in, this fight. The lower self will, for example, whisper that spiritual development effort is futile, that these sought-after states will never be obtained, and that giving up hope is the only justified approach. The lower self acts as though it is a small child, wanting these things to be given to it without any effort, and without having to change. It wants to receive but not to give. The lower self wants a benign and ideal authority to handle these things, wants this authority to do all the hard work for it.

This fight with the lower self involves using positive aggres-sion, which involves taking constructive action with positive intent. Positive aggression also involves fighting for these more evolved spiritual states, and battling for new and better conditions that are compatible with a better world. With the aid of our higher self, our God* connection, this fight involves refusing to succumb to the

---

* If you have not already read the Introduction—where the limitless and unrestrict-ed definition of the Divine is covered—the author strongly urges you to do so soon. Consistent with the instructions in the Introduction, if the use of the word "God" causes some sort of allergic reaction, no matter how subtle, then use your own word(s) instead.

demoralizing and depressing whispers of the lower self. This fight additionally involves a refusal to believe that this self-development effort is futile. The fight involves confronting the attitude that we should simply surrender to the powers of darkness (which can affect us through the lower self). The fight affirms the power of our God connection, affirms the power of our will when it is aligned with God's will, and also affirms the power of our positive thoughts, prayers, and intentions. The fight furthermore involves choosing faith rather than fear, courage rather than cowardice, and the courage to stand up for, and be seen in, God's truth.

To give our very best means that we approach the area of change to which we are committed from all angles. We examine the change we seek to make from all perspectives, considering everything that might need to change, as well as everything that may help bring about and sustain that change. It also means wholeheartedly giving ourselves to this cause. It means that we use all parts of ourselves to work toward the sought-after change. For example, we would then use our intuition, our feelings and emotions, our thinking abilities, our will, our connection with God, our higher self, our skills, and our wisdom.

To give our very best also means that we embrace our work on the change process with dedication and commitment. It means that we use multiple techniques to bring about the change. These include meditation, prayer, visualization, logical investigation of the causes, writing in a journal, seeking counsel from others, and other techniques that may work for us. To give our very best means we create an intense focus that comes together at a single point, centered on the change that we seek to bring about. We give it everything we have; we give it all our energies, and all of our attention. This effort also involves asking God for help in bringing about our presently unmanifested spiritual powers, so that they too might be brought to bear on this change that we so ardently seek.

To give our very best means that our personal will is aligned, on all levels, with the change that we seek to bring about. We must believe that this change is absolutely the best course of action, and that it will benefit all parties involved. Our will must therefore be unbroken by internal forces which oppose the change. To reach this place of inner unity, we must have confronted, resolved, and changed everything inside us that says "no" to the proposed change.

Personal Story:

Werner had been suffering from a series of chronic health problems for several years. These compounded problems started when he first got liver poisoning. As a result of that incident, he almost died in a hospital emergency room. In response to this experience, his body became super-sensitized to many common chemicals such as those in household cleaners, paints, gasoline, perfumes, and even the gasses emitted by new car interiors. When exposed to these chemicals, he would suffer panic attacks, difficulty concentrating, mood swings, insomnia, and ringing in the ears.

He noticed that he was restricting his social activities in order to avoid unnecessary exposures to chemicals. For example, he didn't want to eat out in restaurants, in case they used some unknown ingredient in the food that would trigger his symptoms. He didn't want to visit friends for dinner because he was tired of explaining all the things he couldn't eat, and why he needed to have such strict rules. Besides, he resented having to navigate and address the hurt feelings of the hosts and hostesses at these events. Also, he didn't want to travel, because if he did, he would inevitably be exposed to triggering chemicals such as jet fuel fumes. He didn't want to accept a job in an office building because that would probably include working in a space where chemical janitorial supplies were used, and then the resulting fumes would be recirculated via the air-conditioning system. As a result of all his chemical sensitivities, Werner's life was becoming very narrow and small.

Nobody really understood what was going on with Werner, including his medical doctors, and so he stayed away from them too. Soon he developed a lack of energy, a sore throat, a fever, and a cough that just wouldn't go away. At first he thought it was just the flu, but the trouble continued, and the hacking cough went on for months. Finally he begrudgingly visited his primary medical doctor, who then diagnosed walking pneumonia. His doctor convinced him that it was important to take antibiotics to knock out the pneumonia, lest it turn into something much more serious, perhaps even be fatal.

Not surprisingly, due to his chemical sensitivities, the antibiotic caused serious reactions. Nonetheless Werner completed the recommended ten days of drug therapy. But as a result of the antibiotic, he experienced a resurgence of his serious acute liver poisoning symptoms. Feeling utterly defeated, he felt like crying, like there was nothing he could do, like life was only out to cause him pain and suffering. He felt overwhelmed and unable to deal with all the physical problems coming his way. He briefly considered suicide as a way out of the mess that his life had become.

Werner then began to realize how his feelings—of being totally overwhelmed by problems, of being unable to change anything, of being the victim who had to suffer abuse constantly—were all reenactments of his childhood. He appreciated how these health problems were prompting him to take a new stand for giving his very best to life, to take a stand against his inner child's feelings of hopelessness and helplessness. Werner saw how so much of his life had been structured to avoid feeling helpless and hopeless. He then understood the rightness of all the recent events in his life. He wondered whether these events came into existence so that he might delve deeply into this area where he had for so long feared to go. He also wondered whether these difficult circumstances were in fact a gift from the universe helping him, pushing him, to do the spiritual work he needed to do.

Werner appreciated how life was calling him to step up to a more committed place where he gave his very best, and where he did all that he could, not only for himself, but for his friends, his family, and his neighbors. Werner committed himself to getting out of his childish victimhood. At that point, Werner enjoyed a profound energetic shift, in which he felt newly motivated, more committed to tackle the challenges of life, stronger in his personal fight to give his best, and empowered to create the best that he could in life.

Werner's newly committed perspective caused him to think about how he might isolate the causes of his multiple chemical sensitivities. He decided to keep a detailed daily journal of his activities, his movements, his foods consumed, and his physical reactions. Through the historical analysis that his daily journal provided, he was soon able to identify, and isolate himself from, the situations and chemicals that were causing him distress. He has now resumed the important work projects that were for so long deferred due to his health problems, and he now feels privileged to be able to serve life in this new and more empowered manner.

Journal Questions:

(1) Think back over your life. Make a list of all the important areas where you have given up. In what areas have you allowed the whispers of your lower self to convince you that giving your best is a useless and wasted effort? What exactly were the opposing forces that caused you to give up?

(2) Because you gave up in these areas, make a list of the major opportunities that you missed. Notice how these opportunities were actually within your reach. As you do this exercise, feel how achieving these sought-after objectives was, in fact, not really impossible.

(3) With respect to the single, most important change that you now seek to bring about, to the best of your ability given your current level of consciousness, what are the major opposing forces within you currently saying "no"? Identify each one of these major opposing forces.

3

Identifying with Your Higher Self

Affirmation:

IN PAST MOMENTS of my life, I have known myself as my higher self, that part which is connected to God*. I now choose to ally myself with my higher self. In so doing, I am able to objectively identify the parts of my lower self, as well as how these lower self parts create pain in my life.

Core Idea:

By its very nature, the human personality is split. The personality has a higher self, which is connected with God, and which is already highly evolved. It also has a lower self, which is out of

---

* If you have not already read the Introduction—where the limitless and unrestricted definition of the Divine is covered—the author strongly urges you to do so soon.

touch with God and in a world of separation, misconception, error, and defense.

In a typical human being, these two aspects fight with each other constantly. It is in fact our job in life to purify, educate, and grow up the lower self so that it comes to know truth, comes to know God, comes to know that it is, at its core, made up of the same basic substance as the higher self. It is through this process that the lower self comes to be transformed back into its inherent nature, which is, like the higher self, a divine creation. Said differently, the job that we humans have come to earth to accomplish is to grow up the child inside of us. This is a noble task, an important contribution not only to the consciousness of a particular human being, but to the consciousness of those around that person, and thus also to the consciousness of the world.

The higher self is the most radiant part of a human being's consciousness, and it holds a spark of divine consciousness. The higher self is confident, patient, and imbued with wisdom about what is best for all beings involved—best not only in the short run, but also in the long run. The higher self is the part of us that is in joy, that is already free, that knows the truth, and that knows—and operates in accordance with—the laws of the universe. The higher self is available to all of us, but to reach it, we must first go through our lower self, which has obscured it. Most of us have lost connection with our higher selves, and it is because of this that we have also lost our connection with God. We humans have temporarily cloaked our true nature (godlike) in a denser consciousness associated with the lower self.

The lower self is made up of our faults and weaknesses, including ignorance, laziness, pride, vanity, selfishness, and a desire to have its way without paying the price. The lower self wants to cheat life, wants to take shortcuts without doing the necessary work. The lower self hates to change, and it creates all sorts of denials, resistances, and blockages against any suggestion that it change.

The lower self does not want to admit that it really is like this, and so it adopts a mask that conceals these facts. Recognizing that the exposed lower self is likely to cause trouble with other human beings, we each put on masks that attempt to block others from seeing the truth of our lower selves. Soon thereafter we all start to fool ourselves about the truth of our masks, preferring to believe that our masks are our true selves.

Since the lower self is the part of our consciousness that is clamoring for attention, demanding that its will be done, trying to manipulate others so that it can get what it thinks it needs, it is for most people the part of the psyche to which most people pay attention. Because it gets so much attention, many people erroneously believe that's what they really are, in their deepest essence. We all need to realize that this lower self is simply the temporary cloud that obscures the sun (the latter being the higher self).

To help demonstrate, and later convince ourselves, that we are considerably more than our lower selves, it is important that we repeatedly attempt to get in touch with our higher selves. The higher self, this ever-present, all-knowing, and loving part in each of us is always available. The higher self provides perspective, reframing, and reorientation about the nature of the lower self, which helps us to put the lower self in context. The very act of identifying aspects of our lower self is in fact already a manifestation of our higher self, which is in part the objective observer. When we believe that we are more than our lower self, and when we deliberately seek to connect with our higher self, and when we ask for its guidance, we create a pathway through which the higher self can manifest.

Personal Story:

Mitchell had been out of work for a year. He had been a highly specialized automobile service technician, but his employer of long standing had laid him off. He had not been able to find another comparable job, and he had been living on unemployment benefits and his modest savings while he searched for a position. This went on for eight months. He had lowered his expectations considerably, yet still he could not find a decent-paying job. His situation was partly a reflection of the state of the economy, which at that point was dire. To make matters worse, his retirement account, which was invested in the stock market, had recently suffered very serious losses. Mitchell was gripped by money fears, along with the notion that he would soon be homeless because he would not be able to pay the rent on his modest townhouse.

His mother had recently given him money for living expenses, and he felt embarrassed that he needed a handout. He was full of self-recriminations about not being good enough, about not being worthy of respect. He spent a good portion of his day listening to his inner critic, which had a lot of negative things to say about his value as a man. He even started to believe the condemning words that his ex-wife had thrown at him in the midst of their recent divorce.

Mitchell had become entranced with the messages of the lower self. Although his lower self did seek to protect him by motivating him to quickly get another job, it sought to do this by cracking the whip, and by making him feel like a loser. So far as Mitchell was concerned, at this time in his life, the things he told himself were all true.

One day, a friend of his talked about identifying with himself as "a parent in God." Those words made a lasting impression on Mitchell, and he wondered if he too could step into a place where he knew himself as his higher self, where he could see himself as a parent in God. He meditated and asked God to support him in seeing himself as more than his lower self, as a parent that helped his lower self evolve and come into reality, that is, grow up into adulthood.

In his meditation, Mitchell was delighted that he connected with this sought-after place, and instantly felt much better about his situation. A new and hopeful approach to his difficulties then opened up. Mitchell had energetically tapped into a sense of power and expanded consciousness that felt nourishing and supportive.

He also received a message from his higher self. He heard that his fear meant well, but it really didn't get the big picture, and that was why it was trying to whip him into shape. Mitchell then understood that his lower self was seeking to prevent him from experiencing pain, and the condemnations like "loser," "incompetent," and "stupid" were meant to spur him on. He wrote these words down in his journal and later mulled them over. In the process of examining them, he discovered that they were the same words used by his nosy and meddling grandmother. It was then easy for him to see that these condemning words had nothing to do with his current situation.

He also saw how these words, sourced from his lower self, had caused him great pain and difficulty, how they actually had undercut his confidence during his job search and during job interviews. This new, expanded perspective was useful in that it allowed him to relax about his situation, and allowed him to get into productive action. Soon thereafter, Mitchell was able to land two part-time but good-paying jobs that he still works on to this day.

Journal Questions:

(1) In a quiet meditation, ask for divine guidance, and ask to know yourself as your higher self. See if you can you feel into a deeper place, where you know yourself as both your permanent higher self and your temporary lower self, not just as your lower self. If you can access this place, write a few words about what it's like to inhabit this state, so that you will more readily be able to recreate it at a later time. If you cannot access this place right now, but remember a time when you did, write about that time instead. Repeat the process a few times, until you're in touch with an experience that you know comes from your higher self (based on the feelings of calmness, confidence, groundedness, relaxation, and patience).

(2) Assuming that your task on earth is to transform your lower self, so that it is reeducated in the ways of truth, what is it that your lower self needs to learn now? See if you can go beyond your mask and be honest about the way(s) that the lower self needs to change.

(3) You should know that the lower self is lazy, and that it staunchly resists change. In what way is your lower self now insisting that it not be required to change? Specifically how is this insistence causing trouble and pain in your life?

4

Giving Over to a
Higher Purpose

Affirmation:

I DEVOTE MYSELF to, surrender myself to, and give over to the Creator. I offer all of my life and my energies to further God's work in the world. I set aside my personal preferences, and embrace the will of the Creator.

Core Idea:

Humans are different than other creatures on earth because they have a self-aware intellect. The intellect is a special tool that people have been given so that they can more readily connect with, and align with, the Divine. Use of the intellect for selfish purposes will cause other human gifts to atrophy. For example, employing the intellect to gain material wealth for the sake of gaining power over others is a selfish mis-use of this gift. This is because it violates the truth that we are all interconnected. To misuse the intellect in this way is likely to result in feelings of unhappiness, and an experience of disharmony.

But employing the intellect to gain material wealth to ac-complish some positive community goal, a goal that would not otherwise be possible, would not be a misuse. This ap-proach is likely to result in an inner relaxation and in the unfoldment of additional faculties, such as intuition, in part because the approach is consistent with the unitive and inter-connected nature of the universe.

With the intellect, humans have been given the ability to make their own decisions, to live their own lives. They can choose to live their lives for their own selfish purposes, or for a higher purpose. Seeking to develop oneself, to evolve spiritually, to come closer to God, is a noble higher purpose. Seeking to enrich the world, to bring spiritual truth more vividly into the world, that is also a great spiritual purpose. When one devotes oneself to higher purposes such as these, additional spiritual assistance is mobilized and things that seemed impossible become possible.

Giving over to a higher purpose involves letting go of an insistence that things turn out a certain way. Giving over to God in this way brings with it a neutrality that accepts the will of God, whether or not we personally desire this. When we insist on a particular outcome, when we refuse to accept a certain situation, we make ourselves tense and defensive, and this closes up both the intellect and the mind. When we are neutral, we notice things around us and we are open to the inspiration of the Divine. When we give over to a higher purpose, we invite that inspiration to come into our consciousness.

To be inspired, we need to be willing to go where God seeks to lead us, to be flexible and pliable so that we may readily accommodate new situations. We need to trust our ability to adapt to new situations, knowing that we are supported by and accompanied by the Divine. We need to cultivate the concept that we can be forever ready for something new—knowing that life by its very nature involves constant change.

The intellect, in concert with the will, is an important means to reach a state of advanced consciousness. Its importance should not be denied. The harmonious use of these two faculties is essential for the integration of all parts of the psyche. This harmonious combination can be used to focus one's efforts, to make sense of what's happening, and to reach new conclusions about life. This combination can be used to establish and then follow empowering habits such as meditation. The intellect used in concert with the will can furthermore be used to devote oneself, to surrender oneself, for example, to serving God.

To facilitate constructive change, to move in the direction of creating a meaningful life, a life that is both satisfying and happy, we need to be clear about the objectives that are being served by our intellect. In many cases, simply illuminating the alternative purposes that are served by different courses of action, by different decision options, is a process sufficient to make the right decision clearly evident.

This devotion, this giving over, ideally should be done daily, and in some cases even more frequently. It is a spiritual practice. Like a pianist who practices the scales, who diligently does the exercises that his or her teacher recommends, so do we need to work at this giving over in order to master it. The person who sincerely devotes himself or herself to God will thereby become a channel for insight and inspiration. The intention to be used for a higher purpose, to serve God, assists us in becoming a receptacle, a receiving station, for receiving both inspiration and guidance.

Personal Story:

Veronica grew up in a poor family, and she vividly remembers the deprivation and hunger that went along with the early years of her life. She vowed that she would never again rely on others to meet her needs, because she felt as though her parents had failed her, that they were unable to meet her most basic needs as a child. As a teenager, she set the direction for her adult life by placing her reliance solely in herself, by resolving to do her best to meet her own needs.

She worked hard in school, and got a full scholarship to college based on her diligent and focused work. Her college experience allowed her to develop a high-tech specialty that was in considerable demand. Based on a steady market demand for her services, she set up a small business providing these high-tech services. Over the following years, in some ways her life was rich. She was in fact able to provide for herself, and even bought a house with the money that her small business provided. At the same time, she had no family of her own, and her life seemed dark, narrow, and limited.

After she broke up with her boyfriend, she felt depressed and her life seemed meaningless. She attended a psychology course in an effort to better understand all the many feelings and emotions that were swirling around insider her. She discovered a new fascination with the inner world of people, an interest to which she had not previously given any attention because it was not consistent with being self-sufficient and self-supporting. One course led to another, and soon thereafter she felt called to help others as a professional working in the area of psychology.

While feeling progressively pulled to work in this area, a competing firm approached her and offered to buy her small business. This offer presented a serious dilemma for Veronica. On one hand, the money would help her to get her Ph.D. in psychology and to open up a private practice, a very attractive future direction that she longed to pursue. On the other hand, selling her business made her dependent on a variety of others, including the business buyers, her college teachers, and her future employers. She feared that this dependency would lead to more painful experiences of deprivation, and perhaps even hunger.

She attempted to resolve the dilemma via psychoanalysis, and while the offer to buy the business was still open, she went through an intensive short-term series of therapy sessions. Although the sessions provided some additional information, she still felt inwardly torn. To resolve this dilemma, she then made a pilgrimage to a nearby historic church, and there took a day to pray for divine assistance. In the quiet of that day, she vividly came to understand how holding onto her business was selfish and ego involved, and was intended to protect her from experiencing the pain she went through as a child. On the other hand, she also vividly saw how the money obtained from the sale could finance her graduate studies, as well as finance the development of a new career as a therapist. She then appreciated how selling the business would allow her to surrender to a higher purpose, and would be a way to give more to the world. Based on that new perspective, she sold the business without hesitation, and to this day still enjoys her private practice as a therapist.

Journal Questions:

(1) When it comes to the area of your life in which you would like to change, what higher purpose(s) support that change? Are you willing to give over to this purpose

(or purposes), willing to let go of your personal agenda? If not, why not?

(2) When it comes to the change you seek in your life, in what ways have you been rigid and insistent on a certain outcome? If you were to cultivate an attitude of neutrality, in which you gave over to divine will as it manifests in the truth, how would you then be different?

(3) Take a few moments to meditate: become quiet and empty your mind. Then ask God what his will is for you, in the area where you seek to change. What guidance did you receive? If the answer is not already clear, repeat this same process at some point in the near future, again asking and waiting. If you do this exercise sincerely, you will receive an answer.

5

Dealing with Your Lower-Self Resistance

Affirmation:

I OPEN MYSELF to the bigger picture. I embrace the balanced and all-inclusive truth of the situation that I now inhabit. I choose to set aside all those resistances and reservations about change that do not have a basis in truth.

Core Idea:

Confusion is a tactic used by the "lower self," the latter term being another way to refer to the unevolved aspects inside of us. The lower self employs confusion as a way to keep us stuck, to prevent change and movement. The lower self doesn't want to change because it is lazy. The lower self doesn't want to examine itself because that would perhaps lead to change.

The lower self -- which is made up of faults like fear, self-will, and pride – puts up resistance to the change that we may consciously say we want to undertake. The lower self likes to take the road of least resistance, in which things are left the way they are, or allowed to continue moving in the direction in which they are headed.

Liberation from the oppressive misconceptions of the lower self can only come if we use our conscious will to deliberately examine the nature of our own personal version of the lower self. Only when we use our positive willpower to scrutinize the reasons why the lower self resists change, why it resists revealing itself, and why it wishes to continue its confusions and deceptions, can we start to break the enslaving hold that it has on us.

To facilitate change, the knots and tangles of our personal misconceptions and erroneous ideas about life must be untangled. They must be brought into the light of day and examined, and then challenged, corrected, and reoriented.

The lower self is selfish, preoccupied with its view of reality, and threatened by change. With its very limited and childish view of reality, it believes its role is to protect us. Notice the selfish preoccupation with and exclusive concern about the self, which is a universal characteristic of the lower self. Rather than coming from this default position of self-protection, as is the lower self's habit, we can ask: "What is it that I have to contribute to life, to others, and to God?" With this question in quotes, the limited view of the lower self is reframed, so as to move on to the expansive view of "all of us in this life together." In this reframing we can move beyond the me-versus-the-other perspective and discover possibilities that work for everyone. We can also then explore previously unappreciated solutions to what until now has been our crisis or dilemma.

Such a reorientation takes us out of the little ego, with its selfish concerns, and moves us to a new position where we can more readily connect with our higher self, and thus be able to see the big picture. In this expanded place, we are more likely to empathetically understand why other people are acting the way they are, and to objectively see how our lower self is blocking our own personal evolution.

Personal Story:

Carla had lived in downtown big-city apartments all of her life. These apartments provided a relatively sterile and artificial environment that seemed both dead and dark. For decades she dreamed of moving to the country so that she might have a large garden to grow much of her own food. She yearned for a place where she might connect with nature on a deep and ongoing basis. There was a small town in the country that she often visited on weekend vacations. The town was surrounded by several parks and was right next to the sea. In that place she felt might that she might connect with the Divine through nature. After many years of dreaming about moving there, when she turned fifty-five, and retired from her long-standing corporate job, she finally moved to this little town during the winter.

At this point in her life, she had much to be thankful about. She had a loving boyfriend, a great group of friends, and good health. Although not rich, as long as she maintained a part-time job on the side, Carla had enough money to create her dream living situation, including a large personal organic garden. In many ways she was deeply in touch with how this period in her life was a great opportunity for her to connect with the power to manifest the life she said she wanted.

As expected, the spring after she moved to this little town, she was working in the garden a great deal.

Inevitably, insects come along with gardens. Beetles, earwigs, centipedes, spiders, and a variety of other bugs were all part of the natural scene. Even mosquitoes did not bother her much. But ticks—now they were another story. In ten-day period, she was bitten by two ticks. After the first one bit her, she freaked out. To remove it immediately after she discovered it, she took herself to the local hospital's emergency room at 1:30 AM. She was deathly afraid that she would get Lyme disease, which can be contracted via tick bites. While the use of the emergency room was expedient, it did set her back $500 (she had not yet reached the deductible on her health insurance).

The second time that she got a tick bite, her boyfriend fortunately happened to be visiting, and he kindly and patiently calmed her down, while he removed the tick. Of course, she sent both of these ticks off to a local laboratory to make sure that they did not carry Lyme disease. For each of these tick bites, she also convinced her medical doctor to prescribe a course of antibiotics to make sure that she didn't contract the disease. The up-front antibiotics were not really necessary because Lyme disease was rare in this region. The antibiotics had no real medical purpose, aside from allaying her fears about Lyme disease.

A few weeks later, she was again bitten by a tick. This time it was right between her shoulder blades, in a place that she couldn't reach. Because she was new to the area, she didn't feel comfortable taking her shirt off around other people, and asking them to remove the tick. She thought of asking her best girlfriend, who did live a short drive away, to come over and handle it, but she then remembered that her girlfriend was going out of town that day. She lay awake most of that night with the tick continuing to suck her blood, being particularly aware that she was overreacting, but at the same time still freaking out about the situation.

During that night, Carla prayed that she might understand what it was that the ticks were teaching her. Lying in bed for what seemed like an eternity, she came to understand that she needed to get over her squeamishness, needed to embrace the reality of what it meant to work in a large rural garden. She noted that she felt violated by the ticks, felt like they invaded her body's integrity. She noted that this had a similar feeling to the beatings she had received as a child—a feeling of being punished, but not knowing why she was being punished.

She also came to understand that she had better get used to ticks, because they were part of the garden scene, at least in this region. She also acknowledged that everything on this planet has both good and bad aspects. She furthermore saw how her judgment, about ticks being horrible, wasn't really protecting her much, if at all. From a larger perspective, she saw that she could spoil her own experience of the garden with her tick fears. The next morning she went to a local nurse practitioner and had the tick removed for a very reasonable price. At that point she chose to set aside her fear and reservations about her new garden. This was a relief, because, for the past few months, she had wondered whether she should move back to the big city that she knew so well.

Since that reframing of her situation, new solutions have shown up for Carla. In her relaxation with the presence of ticks, she took a number of preventive measures. Now when she gardens, she tucks her pants into her socks to prevent ticks from getting onto her skin. She also wears light-colored clothing so that she can more readily spot ticks before they bite. She additionally uses essential oils like cedar oil to repel the ticks. Most important, she now grows certain crops that attract quail. A flock of about thirty quail soon took up residence on her property. Quail love to eat ticks. These days, she only gets bitten about once a year, and even then she doesn't freak out. She just does what she needs to do, and doesn't let ticks interfere with her enjoyment of her garden, or with her living her dream in the country.

Journal Questions:

(1) What lower-self resistance do you harbor about making the change you are now considering? Be specific: exactly why is it that your lower self does not want to change? If you can't access this place right now, why is it that you are resisting answering the question? If you find yourself in the latter situation, deal with the resistance first by clarifying it, challenging it, and moving through it.

(2) In what way do these resistances flatter you, for example by making your efforts in opposition to them heroic or super-human? How is your characterization of these resistances deceiving you? Or, using a different vantage point, how is this characterization of your resistances out of touch with reality?

(3) If you were to step back and look at your situation from an objective standpoint, do you really want these resistances to be important and influential considerations that markedly influence the important change that you now contemplate?

6

Recognizing the Spiritual Meaning of Your Crisis

Affirmation:

I AM HONESTLY facing, and asking for God's assistance in learning, what this crisis (or serious problem) has to teach me.

Core Idea:

Crisis occurs when in some way we block the change that needs to take place. With our ego (the part of our consciousness that calls the shots, like a traffic cop directing our lives) we say "no" to a change that must happen. In an attempt to reestablish balance, crisis is telling us that the old structure of our lives must be changed. Crisis is a gift from the universe, tearing down the old structure that no longer works, giving us notice that now is the time to create a new structure that will in fact work.

The old structure that must be torn down is based on one or more false ideas about life, a place where we are not in touch with reality. Crisis is a gift because it's like an earthquake shaking loose those fixed places in our psyches that have become stagnant and unmoving. Life, by its very nature, involves ongoing evolutionary change, so when we do not change along with life, we create a crisis.

Conversely, if we do not resist the change that life is asking of us, we will be free and healthy. If we do not resist change, we can grow and evolve ourselves. But if we have a block, a place where we do not allow the necessary change to proceed, we interfere with the energetic movement of life. The longer and more forcefully we block this energetic movement, the more painful and difficult our circumstances will be. At a certain point, we can no longer bear the pain and difficulty that this blocking creates and, like a burst skin boil, in that moment we are in a full-blown crisis.

If it's not completely addressed, the same problem may come back around again and again. Life will keep giving us painful and difficult situations until we pay attention to the lessons that these situations provide. In fact, the volume of the pain and difficulty associated with these crises will be progressively increased, until we heed the messages and make the required changes. In other words, pain and difficulty bring important messages, and if we ignore these messages, then the spirit world will use still stronger medicine in order to be sure to eventually get our attention. This structure of life is thus for our benefit, because we would otherwise not pay attention to those things which must change, that is those issues on which we need to do some personal work.

Although the metaphorical volume of the pain may be increasing, i.e., although the medicine may be getting progressively more unpalatable -- whether we like it or not -- this process of self-perpetuation of a maladapted and out-of-truth state will at some point have to stop. At a certain point we can no longer avoid facing this pain and difficulty; at some point we can't bear the pain of resistance any longer. We may then have an emotional breakdown, act in a serious and destructive way (perhaps by "freaking out"), or we may be forced to take a significant vacation to reevaluate our life.

Although we may feel as though we are going through a personal failure, we are then at an important inflection point. At that moment we have a chance to change, and a chance to create a new life. Crisis brings a breakdown, but that breakdown also presents us with an opportunity for a breakthrough. The challenge is for us to recognize the signs of trouble, to admit and deal with the pain and difficulty, to identify the messages that are meant for us, and to make the necessary changes, before this destructive process becomes so far advanced that we are in a full-blown crisis. We can, through a cultivated and ongoing personal process of noticing and heeding the signs of upcoming crises, prevent ourselves from suffering the tragedies, interpersonal damages, and emotional upheavals that full-blown personal crisis entails.

If we are going to take a journey by boat—and our spiritual development process can be likened to such a journey—then we must leave the shore where we began in order to get to a different place. We need to arrive at a new place: a new and more evolved place, a place where we have learned the lessons of a crisis. For a while we must be in a no-man's-land, an in-between place, a place where we are simply floating. We must let go of the old ways of thinking, the old ways of unconsciously reacting, and the old ways of doing things. We must tear the old and antiquated structure down, so that something new and better can be built in its place. To admit that what we are doing doesn't work, to affirm that we want to change it, to decide that we can now let go of what doesn't work—those are our commitments to leave the shore where we have been.

Personal Story:

Although he loved her more than any other woman in his life and wanted to be with her, James was terrified of marrying his new girlfriend. He felt torn in two directions: one said, "do it, you won't find a better woman," while the other said, "don't you dare, this will end in disaster." He also felt as though his girlfriend was pushing him into a crisis. After dating for three years, she was feeling her "biological clock" calling her to have children, and she was fed-up with the indecisiveness that James displayed about marriage and children. She had told James that either they got engaged and soon thereafter married, or else she was leaving the relationship. The pressure of her ultimatum upset him and made his indecisiveness still more painful than it had been.

In an effort to unwind the knot of his confusion, James consulted a psychologist. From these meetings, he came to understand that his first wife had been an unusually demanding woman, and that not all women were like his first wife. He brought to vivid consciousness his feelings about his first marriage, in which he felt as though he had become a slave to his wife. James didn't want to repeat the same story with his new girlfriend.

Further personal work helped James see that he was defending himself against women because he believed they all were intent on enslaving him in a marriage. James appreciated how, because of this misconception, he had not been seeing his girlfriend as a unique person. Instead, he saw her as a dominatrix archetype. James admitted that he was overlaying his story about women on top of who his girlfriend really was. At the same time, once he had understood this, he admitted that he had reached a new place of intimacy with his girlfriend, a place where he had never been before, a place where life was asking him to take a leap and embrace a new possibility.

Looking more deeply at this conflict, James realized that he was locked into a pattern where he was imposing his image about relationships between men and women onto his relationship with his new girlfriend. He acknowledged that this imposition was not a loving act; it was instead serving and perpetuating his fear. He saw how he had gotten the idea that wives were demanding, bossy, and dictatorial queens who had to be pleased, no matter what the personal cost to him. As a boy, James felt as though he was forced to cater to his mother's demands, and constantly compromise his own needs and wants, just to get her love and acceptance. Through his work with the counselor, he came to appreciate that nobody required that he cater exclusively to the demands of women, while forgetting his own needs and desires.

With this understanding of the deeper source of his "no," James came to appreciate that there were more than two options: it was not simply a matter of saying "yes" or "no" to his girlfriend's requests for marriage. Instead he could create what for him was a new type of intimate relationship. This could be a relationship in which he stood up for himself, where he let his needs and desires be known, and one in which he negotiated as an equal. From this new way of being, and the ensuing conversations with his girlfriend, he gained a new trust in his girlfriend's positive intentions. More importantly, he also gained a new trust in his ability to speak his truth and stand up for himself. From this new and more trusting place, with both his girlfriend and himself, he was able to later enter into a joyous marriage with this same woman.

From the standpoint of the spiritual meaning of crisis, James' stressful period of indecision was a blessed period. Because he chose to examine the deeper meaning of his troubles, he was able to discover his own misconceptions about relationships between men and women. Since he allowed his life to lead him to what was next in his own personal evolution, he was able to use that situation to help him move to the next level of consciousness. This was a place of conscious creation of his relationship, rather than a place of being forced to decide between two predefined options that had been constructed out of misconceptions regarding past experiences.

Journal Questions:

(1) Looking at your own life, what specifically is the message that this crisis (or serious problem) is asking you to embrace? How is it asking you to change? Be specific about what must change.

(2) What blockage are you creating to the organic and natural movement of your life? In other words, specifically where do you say "no" to this change that needs to take place?

(3) If you release this blockage, if you admit that you can no longer hold back the change that wants to happen, what is it that you fear will happen? Clearly and specifically identify what you fear. Once you have done so, honestly determine whether this result is actually unbearable or unacceptable. Perhaps in reality you can bear it, and you can accept it, even though you don't fully understand what the experience will be like.

7

Failing to Live Up to Your Idealized Self-Image

Affirmation:

I AM HONESTLY admitting and accepting where I am today. I see that I have been harshly judging myself for not being who I have thought I should be. I appreciate that, in reality, I am not required to be that person.

Core Idea:

Life brings us both happiness and unhappiness. Our experience vacillates between the two, and sometimes we even experience both at the same time. We can simultaneously be happy about one aspect of our lives and unhappy about another. To accept that life has both, and that the mixture of both keeps changing, to really get that, and emotionally accept that, opens up an important new door to a different experience of life.

Before we go through this door, we need to acknowledge a childish place in all of us. This place is terribly afraid of unhappiness, and erroneously thinks that if we are unhappy now, then we will always be unhappy. The child in us thus demands that we always be happy. This struggle is tragic because it leads to so much pain and so much unnecessary wasted effort.

The child in us, operating under the erroneous notion that it cannot tolerate unhappiness, unconsciously devises a strategy. When putting together this strategy, the child believes—in its very limited child-logic way of thinking—that this strategy is going to lead to happiness. This strategy can be called the idealized self-image (ISI). For each person, there is a different ISI, intended to create a fantasy set of circumstances that supposedly will lead to our own version of happiness.

One person may think they must be the court jester, forever providing yet another funny joke, because then they can cause others to intently listen to them, thereby getting the attention they missed as a child. Another person may think they must always be compliant and easy to get along with everyone, because then others will want them as lovers, friends, and companions. In that way, they believe they will overcome the loneliness of their childhood. Still another person may think they must understand everything that is happening around them in order to protect themselves from suffering yet another unanticipated attack. If this last person achieves that state of preparation and understanding, then they believe they will no longer suffer the pain of the random acts of physical abuse they experienced as a child.

An idealized self-image is adopted with the intention to avoid unhappiness, because unhappiness makes the child feel insecure and lacking in self-confidence. Turning this around, the child believes that if he or she lives up to the dictates of the ISI, then he or she will experience happiness, security, and self-confidence.

Note that this approach to becoming happy is steeped in duality. In other words, either we are living up to the demands of the ISI, or we are not. Either we are happy, or we are not. In reality, our happiness is a function of our thoughts. If we judge ourselves as failures, we make ourselves unhappy. Under exactly the same circumstances, other people might judge themselves to be successes, and they might then give themselves license to be happy.

Rather than having just two positions, life has many places where our thoughts and feelings can temporarily reside. When we can see how we are making ourselves happy or unhappy, depending on what it is that we are thinking, believing, and/or what we are preoccupied with, then we start to open the door to a new possibility. With this new possibility we can create our own happiness, because we know we can be happy regardless of our circumstances.

It is important that we recognize that happiness obtained because we are living up to the dictates of our ISI is not real happiness but an artificial one. Because this type of happiness is not genuine, the resulting emotional state cannot possibly be as fulfilling as the child within each of us has believed it would be. In support of this, many people who achieve great things, and in the process at least temporarily have lived-up to the demands of their ISIs, will tell you how crestfallen and disappointed they feel, once they achieved their desired goals, the goals that were supposed to make them happy. True happiness comes from other things—like developing one's inherent talents, leading a constructive life, interacting with others in healthy interdependence, and having loving human relationships.

When we act like we have indeed lived up to the most-often-impossible-to-achieve requirements of our idealized self-image, we don a mask. We pretend to be something we are not. Often this mask is consistent with what we were told to be as a child: perhaps perfect, perhaps good, or perhaps holy. If we were not these things that our parents demanded of us, we were punished, or so the child in us thought. Often this punishment included the withdrawal of parental love. As children, we were desperate to regain this love, desperate to once again be happy, and it is with this feeling that the ISI was born.

But in the demand to live up to the perfectionism of the ISI, we create all sorts of trouble for ourselves. To start, we don't give ourselves license to admit and be who we are in this moment. If we do not embrace who we really are right now, if we do not see clearly where we are at this point in time, then we cannot proceed with the changes that life requires of us. If we keep covering up what is true, if we keep putting on a mask, we will disempower ourselves, and block ourselves from starting the necessary process of change.

In a similar way, if we view ourselves as failures, because we clearly do not live up to the dictates of the idealized self-image, then we disempower ourselves. We can then dualistically perform hopeless self-talk such as "what's the use?" We can say things like "why should I care?" even though, on another level, we know that we do indeed deeply care. We can also say "I give up" because the world isn't showing up in a manner consistent with our fantasy dream, expressed as an ISI.

To take back our power, we must never give up on our efforts to obtain what we want out of life. We must keep fighting to conquer untruth and misconceptions, and actively and aggressively investigate what's causing our trouble. To the extent that we give up, or demand that others give us what we must instead give to ourselves, to that same extent do we make our lives futile and meaningless. Likewise, to that same extent do we unnecessarily surrender to a hopelessness based on untruth. We must instead keep going, keep exploring what life is offering to us, all the while recognizing the great power that lies in our thoughts, beliefs, emotions, willpower, and other inner aspects.

Personal Story:

Ian profoundly loved nature and the natural world. As a teenager, he was outraged at how the large corporations were so pervasively "raping and pillaging" nature in the name of profit and progress. After college he joined a famous ecological activist organization that was often in the newspapers because they engaged in high-visibility protests. He was later a crew member on a boat that brought attention to, and interfered with, ships engaged in illegal whaling. One day, while the boat he worked on was docked in the harbor at a major city, a large bomb went off. There was only one crew member on the boat at the time, and that crew member died in the explosion. Ian was elsewhere in the harbor at that time, and was not physically hurt, but his whole view of life dramatically changed at that point.

It soon came to light that a European government military unit had planted the bomb, apparently in support of the whaling companies. In Ian's mind, the bomb represented the triumph of the military-industrial establishment over nature. In Ian's mind, the bomb was a clear statement that all his efforts were for naught, that he was powerless against the vastly more powerful forces intent on destroying nature. Soon thereafter, Ian left the high-visibility ecological organization and became an unemployed alcoholic. It was in drinking that he found a place that allowed him to hide from his pain of being a failure. It was through drinking that he avoided confronting his feelings of hopelessness and powerlessness.

Ian's idealized self-image made very high demands of him. It required that he be a savior, that he have a gigantic impact on the world in order to be both worthwhile and lovable. Ian believed that he had to be the savior in order to really matter, in order to be "somebody" in the eyes of others.

For some time after he left this ecological organization, he took temporary office jobs, so that he could work intermittently, but only as much as he needed to support his very frugal lifestyle. He completely turned his back on the ecological movement, claiming he was disenchanted and had been misled. But really he was only moving to the other end of the spectrum, the other end of his own form of duality. In his mind, either the ecological movement was a powerful savior and therefore consistent with his ISI, or it was a powerless and hopeless sham and therefore inconsistent with his ISI.

To his friends, Ian would often repeatedly complain about how bad people were, how they were dark, cruel, selfish, and hopeless. He would complain about the large corporations, and how they were exploitative, profit-hungry, without a conscience, and leading us all to certain destruction. Although there was some truth behind his complaints, these complaints were primarily projections, ways that Ian was externalizing his own judgments about himself, ways that he was laying the standards of his ISI onto others.

It is a great waste that Ian played the child's game "if we don't play by my rules, I'm going to take my marbles and go home." He is a very intelligent man, a deeply caring man, and a man who could give a great deal to the world. But he is now sidelined, and remains in a no-man's-land, a place of limbo where he beats himself up and repeatedly complains about others. Ian continues to disempower himself through his rigid adherence to the demands of his ISI, perpetuated via his alcoholism, rather than opening up to the opportunities that his life provides.

Journal Questions:

(1) In what specific ways do you now consider yourself to be a failure? In these judgments of failure, what aspects of your idealized self-image are revealed?

(2) In what ways does this idealized self-image demand that you put on a mask to hide the truth? Said a different way, in what ways do you believe you must be good, or perfect, or worthy?

(3) What part in you believes that you are not strong enough to keep confronting this issue, to keep feeling this pain, to keep battling this difficulty? Is its claim to your weakness really true?

8

Noticing How an Image Holds You Back

Affirmation:

I AM NOTICING all the places where I feel blocked and stymied. I resolve to understand, and I ask for Divine assistance in understanding, just why it is that I say "no" to those things that I consciously desire.

Core Idea:

In some cases, even though people have the best of intentions, even though they have great willpower, they are still not able to make the changes that they know they must. They repeatedly attempt to do a certain thing, and repeatedly fail at it, and then stop their attempts, believing that they are unable to achieve the consciously sought-after change. Further attempts are in fact not useless, but before they can be successful, these people need to understand the part in them that is saying "no" to the consciously desired change.

Every person, often in childhood, has adopted certain conclusions about life. These conclusions might be adopted in response to a particular childhood traumatic event, or they might be formed in response to a difficult but ongoing condition facing the child. These conclusions are simply made-up strategies that the child adopted to cope with life, ways that it thought it must protect itself from the uncertainty and difficulty of life. These conclusions were unfortunately made with child consciousness, more specifically an incomplete understanding about the nature of life. These conclusions were also the result of emotional reactions, rather than an objective and logical analysis of the reality of the situation. As a result, these conclusions often take the form of "I must" have an experience that is the opposite of what was experienced as a child. These conclusions—you can call them images about life—then become general rules defining how things must be.

Every life has its hardships, its difficult moments, its challenges, but how a person deals with these is critical. If these are met with rigid rules about how things have to be, "images" if you will, then the life experience of the person involved is going to be quite painful. On the other hand, if a person can show up in the truth of the moment, can flexibly bend and change in light of this truth, life will not only be much more enjoyable, but change can be embraced as a natural aspect of everybody's life. If God is always changing, and if people are extensions of God, then people are always changing too. But if images demand that a life experience show up in a certain fixed way, and if the circumstances do not readily support that experience, there will be serious trouble.

In order to accelerate our own personal evolution, we need to do three things: (1) meet the truth of the moment with a relaxed acceptance, (2) be willing to rapidly and adaptively change our circumstances in response to new information, and (3) emotionally keep moving with, and growing in response to, the flow of what life brings to us. Images are like dams in the Divine flow of life, and they block the movement that wants to take place, and as a result they cause puzzlement, anxiety, fear, and disorder. The flow can only be reestablished after a person explores that part of his psyche that says "no," understands why this negating image was adopted, and sees that the image no longer serves him or her.

In many cases, images are found in the unconscious, and as long as they remain there, they cannot be changed. By looking at the circumstances of our lives, we will see patterns that indicate the presence of an image. For example, if a particular woman genuinely and fervently wished to experience exactly the opposite of what she experienced, but the undesirable experience is nonetheless repeated anyway, this is a good indication that an unconscious image exists. For all of us, this place in the unconscious is not logical, it is made up of child consciousness, and as such, it does not realize that this image blocks the very experience that we consciously seek.

Personal Story:

Wolfgang had two houses, one in the city and one in the country. This arrangement worked well for him for many years, because he had the income from a building construction-related job to support two houses. When the economy took a serious downturn, he was distressed to find that there were no takers for his construction services. He did the calculations and discovered that consolidating into one house, notably his house in the country, could save him forty percent of his monthly expenses.

He then resolved to make the move out of his city house, but delayed his follow-though on the plan for months. Friends and business contacts would ask how he was doing with the move, and he would reply that he was still "in process." After another six months had elapsed without any substantial work on the move away from his city house, as his bank account was running dry, and as he was forced to borrow money on his credit cards, he finally admitted that something big was blocking him from proceeding.

Accustomed to using his will to push himself to do things, he started packing up some of his belongings in boxes. He was then surprised to notice overwhelming feelings of sadness and grief. He thought these feelings were important, so he took a break and wrote in his journal, asking God for assistance in understanding how he was blocked with the move. He then realized that he was still holding onto the prospect of getting back together with his ex-wife. He had lived with his ex-wife some eighteen years earlier in the same city where his city house was located. As he and his ex-wife had argued about money and other things, he had moved out of their shared house and into his nearby office, to let her cool off. When things calmed down a bit, he would try to move back in with her. He repeated this process five times, eventually giving up on her when she became seriously violent during an angry outburst.

At the time of all those arguments, Wolfgang had rented an office across the street from his current townhouse. When the landlord sold that office, he had simply moved about a half-block away, all the while unconsciously still waiting to reconcile with his ex-wife. Now he understood why he had not previously moved away from that city, and why he was having so much trouble moving to his country house.

On a deep and unconscious level, Wolfgang believed that he had to be patient, had to play the role of the peacemaker, because this is what he had done to restore normality in the chaotic environment of his nuclear family's household when as a child. When he was able to let go of the image of waiting to reconcile with his ex-wife, when he admitted that it wasn't going to happen, when he understood that he didn't even consciously want this reconciliation to happen, then he was able to rapidly and efficiently pack up his stuff and make the move to his country house.

Journal Questions:

(1) For a moment, quietly feel into your inner reaction to the change you wish to make. Notice the feelings and thoughts that come up. With regard to this change, is there a particular fault that you don't seem able to overcome, in spite of genuinely wanting to do so? (Faults are aspects of the lower self and they include: pride, fear, self-will, selfishness, envy, greed, revenge seeking, stealing things, telling lies, vanity, egotism, laziness, unjustified stubbornness, denial of the facts so as to remain ignorant, refusal to take personal responsibility, and inventing excuses to remain an emotional child.) In your journal, describe this particular fault and why you are apparently not able to change it. What specifically in you is saying "no" to changing this fault?

(2) In what way is this fault a defense for you? How do you protect yourself with this fault? Is there an image about how you have to be that incorporates this fault?

(3) Are there repeated incidents in your life where this fault, and its associated image, come to the forefront of your consciousness? What are the common factors found in all of these incidents? And in each of these incidents, is there a similar way that you are out of touch with the truth?

9

Coming Out of Denial and Going Beyond Your Mask

Affirmation:

I EMBRACE THE temporary truth of the unpurified parts of my personality. I can admit what's true because these parts are, in their essence, only Divine parts which are in error, parts that have lost their way.

Core Idea:

Beyond the higher self and the lower self, there is another level of consciousness that human beings adopt. That is the mask—what we pretend to be, but in truth are not. When a child realizes that certain aspects of his or her lower self may cause conflict with others, he or she cloaks this part of the personality. The child is not ready to pay the price, not ready to evolve these parts, and not ready to suffer the consequences of living authentically. In that moment, the child makes a decision about himself or herself, a decision to hide, and tries to appear to be better than he or she really is. The child chooses not to confess the truth, not to change, and not to wrestle with the lower self as it really is. In large measure because the lower self is still unknown and unseen, the child believes that all he or she can do is to hide those parts that appear to be unacceptable.

When the child adopts a mask, it chooses to sell out to short-term convenience, at the cost of long-term pain and difficulty. From the place of child consciousness, the place of an undeveloped and limited viewpoint, the mask seems to be a convenient mechanism to avoid a wide variety of difficulties, unpleasant situations, and disadvantages. For example, with the mask, a person may falsely act unselfishly, when underneath he or she is driven by selfish motives. This could happen if the person was looking to impress others with their apparently unselfish behavior. This pretentious behavior in turn creates an inner war in the psyche of all those who adopt this strategy. In this unnecessary war, the person is torn between two opposing strategies. On one hand, the person believes that they must compulsively do what they feel (for example, act selfishly). On the other hand, the person feels they must do something else in order not to be ostracized and rejected (for example, act unselfishly).

When people have masks, they make their lives a lie, and in the process they alienate themselves from whom they really are.

After a while they start to believe that they are their masks. The true nature of the lower self is lost from the forefront of their consciousness. This awareness gradually falls into the subconscious, and this in turn makes the truth of what's really happening all the more difficult to access. As this self-alienation becomes more entrenched in the personality, people often feel as though they are a fraud, as though they are unworthy of love, and/or unworthy of the abundance that the universe wants to give them. This is in part because they are attempting to trick others into giving them what they want via false pretenses.

The more that people push away, and refuse to look at certain aspects of their lower selves, the more difficult it will be to heal and evolve these parts. These lower-self aspects are in error, simply mistaken about the true nature of reality. Like the rest of the personality, in their essence these parts are Divine consciousness. These parts have simply become blinded, separated, and lost from their connection with the Divine. These childish parts can mature and then be reintegrated with the rest of the personality, but this can only happen when these parts are truthfully acknowledged, genuinely accepted, and worked with in a dedicated fashion.

Personal Story:

Madeline grew up in a household with two brothers, and no sisters. As the eldest, she was often expected to take care of the other children. Because she was very bright, she was perceived by her parents to be self-sufficient and mature beyond her years. As a result, Madeline received very little attention and protective care from her parents. In reaction, she became angry about what seemed to be a great amount of attention and parenting that her brothers received, attention way beyond that which she received. To conceal this anger, and in the hope of obtaining her parents' love, she adopted a mask of being bright, self-sufficient, and competent.

The adoption of this mask had its own negative consequences. The more Madeline acted as though she was bright, self-sufficient, and competent, the less help and support she got from others. This result was initially created with her parents, but it later applied to her relationships with friends, other family members, work associates, and lovers. This result in turn created a vicious circle in which she believed that people would not be there for her, where she was therefore forced to be still more self-reliant, self-supporting, and self-soothing. As time wore on, she became very angry about this issue, and soon believed that people weren't going to be there for her—ever. For example, she would call her family every day, subtly looking to receive support and parenting, but instead often ended-up providing the support and caring that she sought.

After her boyfriend broke up with her because he felt that he could contribute nothing to her, Madeline sought some counseling assistance. Through this counseling work, it came to light that her mask made her resistant to accepting the support and loving attention of others. Her boyfriend felt blocked, as though he couldn't deeply reach her, in large part because she was unable to drop her mask of the independent and self-sufficient provider of support. When she was able to embrace herself as a normal person, an ordinary person who needed love and support, as well as attention and care, then she allowed herself to receive what she needed from others in a way she had not since childhood. This new willingness to receive in turn created an opportunity for intimacy that had not previously existed.

Madeline began to open up emotionally in a new, deeper, more receptive, and more fulfilling relationship with a new boyfriend. This boyfriend was very self-revealing emotionally, and he was delighted that Madeline shared so much of her inner process with him. He was also pleased that Madeline was willing to receive his suggestions, his loving concern about her, and other types of offered support. The deep sharing that they had with each other, in fact, fueled the fires of passion, and made them both more interested in being together.

Journal Questions:

(1) Define the mask that you have adopted. In what ways do you feel as though you must present yourself to others? Looked at another way, in what ways do you want people to see you, even though you know these ways aren't really true? To have resistance to this particular question

is natural, but see if you can stay with it long enough to come up with a list of five to ten aspects of your mask. One example of a mask: "I know the answer, I know what's happening now and in the future, I have everything handled, I am the authority, and I am always right."

(2) After you have listed a number of different aspects of your mask, define the specific corresponding lower-self traits (you could call them faults) that your mask conceals. Note that there is likely to be a direct correspondence, perhaps even a direct opposition, between aspects of the mask and aspects of the lower self. For example, a mask of unselfconscious giving and compassion might conceal a fault of selfish preoccupation.

(3) Realistically, what would happen if other people knew about these same lower-self traits identified via the prior question? Would such a disclosure actually be as terrible as you make it out to be? Why is it that you have invested so much time and energy in this mask? Is all this time and energy really warranted?

10

Getting That Your Thoughts Create Your Reality

Affirmation:

MY EXPERIENCE IN life is a direct result of the thoughts I have. I ask for Divine assistance in my efforts to notice how my thoughts create my reality. Help me to be attentive to my inner reality, so as to consciously register even the most fleeting of thoughts.

Core Idea:

Humans are physically oriented. The reality of the body and its functions, as well as the reality of what humans can feel and touch, dominates human consciousness. This physical orientation leads people to believe that the physical is what matters, and is what is real. But what is physical is in reality the result of consciousness. Consciousness, taking the form of thoughts and feelings, creates the physical world. The physical world is the effect, and the inner world (such as thoughts and feelings) is the cause. Most people have this reversed; for example, they believe that if the physical world is changed in a way more to their liking, then they will be happy.

The relationship between cause and effect is confused for many people because they do not yet see the connections between their thoughts and feelings and the external world in which they live. This difficulty is in part a reflection of the fact that the physical world slows down the process of creation. In the spirit world, there is an instant creation in response to a thought and/or feeling. In the material world, it may take a long time before a thought and/or feeling creates a specific result. The often long and drawn-out process makes it more difficult for people to put the pieces together, but the pieces can nonetheless be readily connected, at which point the individual involved can start to operate more at the level of cause, rather than effect, in his or her own life.

While these ideas may at first seem difficult to understand, they are nonetheless very powerful. Like all material in this book, don't believe a word of it just because it's written here. Try it out in the world. Engage in an experiment, apply these ideas to your life, and you will most likely notice that your experience of life is markedly different. This book will be of no use to you if you don't seriously and diligently apply these ideas to your personal life. Here we have an example of what was mentioned above. Your life will not change unless you change your thoughts and feelings. If you don't give the material in this book a chance, then the change that you so ardently seek will certainly have no chance of materializing. But if you do shift your inner world, if you do adopt some different thoughts and feelings, then the outer world will soon follow suit.

Taking this discussion one step further, it can be said that the world is illusory, a mirror of the thoughts and feelings that we have. The real world is the world of consciousness, the world within us, all of us. While we as human beings cannot fully understand the nature of the spirit world, we can get glimpses of it in meditation, in prayer, in nature, and in moments of epiphany when we sense the interconnectedness of everything (or All-That-Is). The more we can open to this world of spirit, or the world of consciousness, the more we come into reality. Said differently, the more we can heal our erroneous concepts (which have been helping to cause both emotional reactions as well as unpleasant circumstances), the more we are able to connect to the true reality. It is the healing of erroneous concepts, and the opening to our innate power to create the life that we yearn for, that this book is focused upon. The first step in this process is the transformation of unreality, the shifting of disempowering and erroneous concepts.

Reality is the truth, but this is not the superficial truth, the truth based in the material world alone. Reality is the deeper all-encompassing truth, the level at which things are all connected, the level at which things are sourced. The more you are in true reality, the better will be your comprehension of the workings of cause and effect in your life. A simple example will illustrate this point. If someone insults you, making unfair accusations, you may feel hurt. It is true, on a superficial level, that you are feeling hurt. And as long as this is the extent of it, you will probably remain hurt, at least for a short time. But the deeper truth includes the motivating connections that led up to this hurtful event. There may be some good reasons why this person insulted you. If you are willing to honestly search for and reflect about these reasons, you have a chance of understanding the deeper truth, the truth that actually sourced this event. If you can go to this place, and learn from it, the hurt will be healed; this healing comes about in part because you have taken responsibility for your co-creation of what happened. If you do this work, you will emancipate yourself from your own self-imposed unreality, and thus the reality of you as the creator of your own experience will then be progressively revealed.

Most human beings go through life passively, at the effect of their thoughts and feelings (the latter simply being unthought thoughts). In this respect, these people do not firmly grip the rudder and steer the boat of their lives. For example, if a man thinks that he is not "good with numbers," his life will show up like a self-fulfilling prophecy. Sure enough, he will have difficulty with his taxes, with his bank account reconciliation, and with other matters involving numbers. It is a whole lot more fun and desirable to be the cause of something, than it is to be at the effect of something.

It is in fact possible to choose to have certain thoughts. All of us can choose right now to have thoughts that are in truth, thoughts that are loving, and thoughts that are constructive. We can bring these thoughts to bear on our personal process regarding the change we seek.

Thoughts of truth allow us to confront those places in our inner world that are unrealistic. Thoughts of love will allow us to appreciate that we are absolutely worth the investment of time and effort it takes to bring about a lasting and fundamental change in our lives. Thoughts of positivity will affirm our faith that we will in fact be shown, by Divine guidance, the next step in our own personal change process. With these thoughts we help clear away the unreality that obscures how we are the creators of our own experience in life.

Personal Story:

Trudy had three small children at home, and next to no support—financial or otherwise—coming from their father. As the father of her children, she had chosen a man who was totally uninterested in being a father, a man who was unemployed and chronically poor. To try to get him to live up to what she thought he should do as a father, she would nag him, threaten him, and shame him. It was therefore understandable that, because of his lack of support for the family, she suffered with a great deal of tension, strain, anxiety, and upset. Trudy was attempting to impose a certain set of expectations on a man who was utterly uninterested, and had been that way for a long time—in fact all the way back to the point in time when she first met him. To the extent that Trudy thought she was going to change him, Trudy lived in unreality.

Through the graciousness of a friend, she was able to get some free babysitting support. This enabled her to get away from her kids for a while, so that she could attend a class. In the class, there were five other women students, and one lifelong-bachelor middle-aged male student. In the first class, she said to the man that she "wanted to kick him in the shins." Taken aback by this statement, the man asked her to explain why she would say that to him, because he had just met her for the first time in the class, and she knew nothing about him. Trudy was taken off guard by his question, because she had expected him to be defensive rather than inquisitive. In her confusion she offered some remark about how she would feel more comfortable in a class that was all women, and let it go at that. But the tension with this male student remained.

In a subsequent class, out of the blue, she accused the male student of being "deceptive," and this too, puzzled the man. He asked Trudy in what way she thought he had deceived her. She stumbled with her words, and couldn't come up with anything from this lifetime. She alleged that he had deceived her in a prior life. In response to this, the man claimed that she couldn't realistically expect to hold him accountable for something that he didn't remember, something allegedly from a prior lifetime. Nonetheless, Trudy maintained her tense, hostile, and accusatory position. The man then asked her if perhaps he reminded her of another man in her present life.

All of a sudden, Trudy had a rush of understanding. She felt about this man the same way she felt about one of her brothers. When she was six years old, this brother had told Trudy that he would keep a secret of hers, and that she could safely tell it to him. That brother went on to tell other people her secret, and she was hurt, and later humiliated by the revelation. She explained to this fellow student that she believed that her brother had deceived her, and that he all along intended to tell her secret to other people. The male student asked Trudy to consider the possibility that perhaps her brother did not intend all along to deceive her. Perhaps, said the man, her brother was tricked into revealing the secret. As Trudy considered the possibility that her brother may not have had a premeditated intent to deceive her, the male student wondered out loud whether Trudy might have a belief that men will deceive her.

In large measure because she was looking honestly at the reason she was treating this man inhospitably, she overcame her own resistance to the truth about her actions. A deeper level of truth opened up at that point for Trudy. She understood that she wanted men to live up to her criteria of what a good man should be. Her own father had not been there for her mother, a woman who raised several small children largely on her own in a poor and difficult situation – a scenario not far different from the one of Trudy's present experience. Trudy deeply yearned to have a man be what she had been told good men should be, specifically providers for and protectors of the family. Since the men in her life were not the way she thought they should be, to her that meant that they were "deceptive."

In that moment Trudy understood that the reason she had resented all men was because she had not had the type of father others seemed to have had. She understood the beauty of her spiritual process, and how choosing a certain man to be the father of her children had helped to lead her to this realization. In that moment a new and more open-minded way for Trudy to relate to men was revealed. In that moment she could allow men to be who they actually were, instead of trying to mold them to suit her notion of who they should be for her.

Journal Questions:

(1) What thoughts have you had about your personal process surrounding the change that you hope to make? (For example, "it's hopeless.") What reality would these

thoughts most likely create? (For example, they might create "a complacency with a painful and undesirable situation.") Make a table with at least five rows and two columns. Put five separate thoughts about your personal process in each of the rows of the first column. Then put the resulting likely-to-occur creations in the second column across from each of these thoughts.

(2) Imagine that you were in a position of powerful self-creation, in other words, that your life was self-created in a supportive and constructive manner. Under those imagined circumstances, what then would your thoughts be? Make a list of at least ten positive thoughts in your journal.

(3) Assume for a moment that the process of making this sought-after change is itself a significant spiritual teaching for you. With that assumption, which thought might your higher self have had, so that your current change process would then be prompted to occur? In other words, if you were coming from a higher-self place (an evolved, all-knowing, loving, open, truthful, relaxed, patient, and constructive place), and you were designing your own personal development process, what would your strategy be? Seriously engaging with this question can help to reframe the change process as a desirable and constructive evolutionary sequence, something blessed and natural, and most important something you can consciously direct.

11

Making an Inventory of Your Faults

Affirmation:

I SURRENDER TO the truth as life presents it to me. I challenge those parts of myself that stubbornly refuse to admit, and learn from, the truth. I am coming to appreciate that there is nothing to fear about the truth, and that the truth can set me free.

Core Idea:

Every human being has a lower self, a part of their psyche that is still a child, that is blind and in darkness, and that is self-centered and out-of-touch with reality. Part of our task on earth, as human beings, is to grow this lower self up, to reeducate it, to evolve it, to transform it, so that it returns to its original nature, which is simply a particular ray of light, another manifestation of God.

One of the greatest hindrances to achieving this reeducation process, or blocks to completing this transformation process, is our stubbornness. This stubbornness could be about anything: perhaps resistance to the painful truth of our current situation, perhaps resistance to understanding the importance of taking responsibility for what has happened, or perhaps our resistance to letting in the reality of the pain we have caused others (especially when our lower self has acted out).

Stubbornness is particularly problematic when it manifests as an unwillingness to understand something that has happened in our lives, when it shows up as our unwillingness to put together cause and effect. To see our personal influence, to understand the different aspects of our lower selves, to acknowledge how our un-evolved parts may have been partially to blame for an undesirable situation—all of these require that we give up our stubbornness.

It is not enough that we live what many would consider to be decent lives, and that we abide by the laws of the land. If we want to emotionally and spiritually evolve, we need to identify the aspects of our lower selves, and we need to see how these aspects operate in our lives. We also need to consciously choose not to favor or acquiesce to the demands of these still-unevolved parts of ourselves. This growing-up process will help us to overcome the self-made chains that now encumber us. This process will help us to create one or more new possibilities, which in many instances had not previously presented themselves to us (or at least we didn't notice them).

So, if you really want to change your situation, a good start would be to prepare a comprehensive inventory of your faults. Being as objective as you can, see the many ways that you resist life, and the ways that you stubbornly say "no" to the truth. It is important that you write down this list, because the lower self wants to remain in darkness, wants to keep these things away from scrutiny, because the lower self does not want to change (the lower self is lazy).

You cannot successfully fight with your lower self, and then evolve it—for example by showing it a better way to be—if you don't already intimately know your lower self. The lower self can be readily illuminated by closely examining those areas where you are having trouble in life. If you are experiencing difficulty somewhere in life, then some aspect of your lower self must be at work there.

The lower self is made up of fear, self-will, and pride, and all the variations that go along with these three larger categories. For a moment, because it's relevant to our personal development process, let's look at a subcategory of pride. One aspect of our lower self might be the fear of looking stupid and dumb. And this lower-self aspect might cause us great trouble if our job requires that we regularly make speeches to large numbers of people. Similarly, if we feared that someone might discover our personal journal, where a list of faults appeared, and that by this discovery we might then look bad in their eyes, then we might, if we sold-out to this type of pride, refrain from undertaking this important listing of our faults.

Everything that we suffer from is caused, in whole or in part, directly or indirectly, by our shortcomings, by our faults. Although it may not at first seem likely, the preparation and expansion of this list of faults will help to emancipate you. Your stubbornness and resistance to even doing this exercise is an indication of your lower self at work. Look at this stubborn reaction, and ask for Divine guidance about this, ask to know this part that keeps refusing to conform to the truth.

Personal Story:

Early in her career, Yvonne had worked for nearly twenty years at a lobbying firm in the capital of a large and prosperous country. She loved her job as an animal rights activist, and she developed many deep friendships with coworkers during that period of time. Because she had to make more money to support her family, she quit that job five years ago.

Yvonne woke-up one morning thinking of a close friend and former coworker, a woman she knew from her former job in the capital, a woman who had fought breast cancer with chemotherapy. Although the cancer had been cured, her friend, Christine, had later contracted leukemia from the chemo treatment she had earlier received. Yvonne remembered how the battle against the leukemia had been difficult for Christine, and how Christine had led an amazing life as an animal champion throughout it all.

Yvonne had been more in touch with Christine during the past few months of her life, and sent her healing prayers from time to time. The day before she engaged in these ruminations, Yvonne received an email from a mutual friend, an email indicating that Christine had taken a dramatic turn for the worse, and that she was not likely to live through the end of the week. Yvonne then was overtaken by a sense of having missed out on what might have been a great relationship with Christine.

Yvonne felt her sadness that she had not honored Christine more fully while she was on the earth. Yvonne had not allowed herself to develop a deeper friendship with Christine, because she was too stubborn to let go of her anger about an old wound. Many years ago, when Yvonne's husband had died, Christine had seemed illusive and unavailable to Yvonne. At that time, Christine was so focused on saving the animals that she didn't realize how her words and actions affected Yvonne. At that time, Yvonne was more of a shell of who she had been, rather than the vibrant and passionate co-warrior to whom Christine had become accustomed. Yvonne felt remorse about the way she still harbored resentment toward Christine, about the way she had steadfastly refused to release that resentment, and had thereby blocked herself from opening to a loving place with Christine. Yvonne deeply felt how this stubbornness of hers had caused her a big loss, a great missed opportunity. Yvonne also then became crystal clear about the fact that this loss was something that she alone had created.

Yvonne thought about how much she could have learned from Christine. Yvonne went over the many ways she could have grown from a deeper relationship with her, if in no other way than learning the importance of forgiveness. Yvonne wondered what might open up in her life as a result of dropping her stubbornness, even though a relationship with Christine was clearly no longer possible.

Journal Questions:

(1) Make a comprehensive list of your faults, as you now understand them. You can start by listing all the areas where you are having trouble in your life, and then ask: "What might the fault be that is contributing to this trouble?" Be as clear and undisguised as you can be. Write objectively about your lower self as though you were a concerned and loving third person. (Note that this list can be, and ideally should be, expanded upon every so often, so as to widen your self-understanding and self-knowledge.)

(2) Show your list to a close friend or loving relative, somebody who knows you well, and then ask them to help you expand the list. Let them know that you won't be angry with them, or hurt by them, when they help to identify your faults. Genuinely help them to understand that their feedback will assist you, and that you will seriously consider what they have to say. Try, as best you can,

not to react negatively when they offer ideas. Simply listen appreciatively, and later take this information calmly into your meditation. Be sure to diligently write down all the faults that they mention. If you have resistance and a stubborn refusal even to consider this step, again look at what aspect of the lower self might be influencing your position here. Might that part be a certain vanity, or perhaps a bit of oversensitivity to looking bad?

(3) If you feel even slightly disinclined to undertake the preparation of an inventory of your faults, ask yourself: what is this part that says "no"? Affirm your intention to evolve, to align yourself with the truth, to know God's will for you. From what part of your lower self are you finding a refusal, and a stubborn resistance? Can this same resistance be found in your unwillingness to honestly and objectively understand both cause and effect in the area of your life that now troubles you most?

12

Meeting the Fear You Don't Want to Feel

Affirmation:

I AM NOW feeling all of my feelings and learning what they have to teach me. Whatever the feeling, I can bear to feel it. After I feel and experience it, it will soon change, and I will then come out on the other side.

Core Idea:

Fear that is not fully and squarely met is debilitating. Fear that is not challenged, fear that gets puffed up way out of proportion by our imagination, ends up running our lives. One of the most serious fears is the fear of feeling a particular feeling.

If we are in real danger, perhaps because a large and dangerous wild animal is attacking us, there is something specific that we can do about it. For example, we can run away. But fear of our own feelings, unless it is identified and challenged, can't actually be dealt with. As long as fear of a feeling is denied, and the topic is pushed out of our conscious minds, it only remains in a stuck and painful place, until the time comes when we are finally willing to deal with it.

When we fight against feeling one of our feelings, we create suffering for ourselves. When we say to ourselves, "No, I can't feel that feeling again," we establish a duality. Part of us then has a yes-current (I am able to feel this) and another part of us has a no-current (I am not able to feel this). As long as we avoid honestly looking at this matter, we perpetuate our own suffering. As long as we avoid challenging this duality, we make ourselves tense, because the no-current pushes against what is true (the yes-current).

We can create a new and more empowered way to be when we allow ourselves to feel all of our feelings. Our feelings, by their very nature, will organically change and evolve, if we don't hold them back with our no-current. When revealed and challenged, the no-current be shown to say untrue things like "No, I will die if I feel those feelings again." When we stop guarding against our feelings, we engender an open and relaxed inner state that allows us to be more creative about the problems we face. When we allow these feelings to be felt and experienced, we move with the stream of life, and start to see new possibilities that we had not seen before. It is then that we can perceive the possibility of a positive change, the outlines of a new way to be.

An open and relaxed energetic approach to life is also conducive to pleasure, joy, and fulfillment. Then we have the flexibility to go where life wants to take us. But if we resist a feeling, we create an overactive mind. This overactive mind wastes a great deal of our life energy trying to arrange our life circumstances so that we do not need to experience the feared feelings again. Our minds for example can build cases against other people, blaming them for forcing us to feel the undesirable feelings, when instead we should be taking self-responsibility.

If we don't do this inner work, our overactive minds create reasons why we shouldn't have to feel these feared feelings. These, and other excuses justifying our fear, are all illusions. The more we indulge in these illusions, the more precarious we feel about our life, because we are relying on our minds alone, when we should instead be relying on all of our inner resources, including our feelings. These mental constructs, invented to support our fear of our feelings, aren't even convincing to us because they feel sterile and lacking in aliveness. We can regain our balanced and integrated selves, but only if we allow our feelings to be fully felt and experienced.

Personal Story:

Pamela entered a convent straight out of college. After spending a few decades there, a priest told her that she needed to leave, needed to go out into the world and have a life of her own. She followed his advice, and soon became a highly sought-after kind of spiritual teacher for youth who were in trouble, working in several public schools as circumstances with these young people required. But after five years out of the convent, she was not able to properly manage her money, and she found herself being forced into bankruptcy by her creditors.

At this point, she called-up one of her former boyfriends, a man she briefly dated after she left the convent. She hadn't spoken to him for three years, but now she was surprisingly flirty and chatty. After a while she told him that she was in serious financial trouble, and that she needed him to bail her out. Her ex-boyfriend Victor objected to a number of the assumptions behind her pleas.

First, Pamela assumed that Victor owed her something because he was her ex-boyfriend. He claimed that he owed her nothing, and this infuriated her. Second, she thought that he should give her the money she requested because he had more money than she did. He told her that he didn't believe that being more affluent was a compelling reason either, and that response infuriated her still more. Third, she claimed that it was his job to take care of her because he was a man. Victor also didn't buy that argument, reminding her of all the things she had once said about gender equality. Her anger, at that point roaring, tipped Pamela off that a significant personal issue was in play.

Victor went on to inform her that she wasn't a good risk, especially because she was likely to soon go into bankruptcy. After a drawn-out verbal fencing match, he did eventually agree to give Pamela a small, interest-free loan that was fully secured by her car, which had fortunately been paid off some time ago. She didn't like the terms, but because she was desperate, Pamela accepted the offer.

Three months later, Pamela was drawing up the papers for bankruptcy, and she noticed that she was required by law to list all of her debts. She didn't want to put the loan from Victor down on the list, because she believed that the court would probably sell her car in order to satisfy the loan to Victor. She called Victor again, and tried to get him to convert her loan to a gift. Another extended conversation ensued, and it then came to light that she thought Victor had an obligation to take care of her and protect her—even though he was no longer her boyfriend. He refused her pressure to turn the loan into a gift. Pamela then arranged for one of her women friends to pay off Victor before the court hearing, so that she didn't need to list this loan in her papers, thus allowing her to keep her car.

The discussions with Victor, and the financial crisis surrounding her bankruptcy, caused Pamela to really closely look at what was going on in her life. Through this very painful series of events, she came to appreciate that she was afraid of feeling sadness, specifically the sadness associated with her very difficult childhood. Both of her parents were irresponsible drug addicts and had not been available for her when she was growing up. Her father spent many of her childhood years in jail. Taking this process still deeper, through an intensive self-examination process occurring right after the bankruptcy, Pamela saw how desperate she was not to feel the excruciatingly painful sadness about the childhood that she never really had. Since her parents weren't available to do the childrearing work, Pamela had been forced to take care of her younger sister, even though she herself was still a child.

Pamela also saw how she had created many reasons why it was the responsibility of others for her not to feel this sadness. She also noticed how hard she was working at not feeling the displaced feelings that went along with this sadness, notably self-pity, despair, and hopelessness. She had made Victor responsible for protecting her from these feelings, and she had justified her own maneuvers to avoid feeling that sadness. For example, going into the convent had been a solution of sorts, a way for her to put something big (like God) in between her and the feared feelings of sadness.

For the first time in her life, she allowed herself to fully feel the feelings that she had been terrified to feel. Pamela appreciated that it was time she came to terms with the pain of her childhood. Although some people said she couldn't afford it, she took several weeks off from work, to allow herself to go through this sadness, to allow herself to be with the feelings that she had imagined she couldn't handle, to come to a new place where she felt cleansed and empowered. This confrontation of the truth, and the process of going through her feared feelings, gave her a new sense of personal confidence, which she is now using to create a new type of progressive school for children who have been in trouble with the law.

Journal Questions:

(1) What precisely is the feeling experience against which you guard and defend? In other words, what pain have you decided you cannot feel? (Underneath several layers of consciousness, it is a pain that you believe you cannot bear.)

(2) Specifically what will happen if you experience those feared feelings? Is this experience really as catastrophic as part of you makes it out to be?

(3) This question involves closing your eyes, imagining a possible scene in the future, writing a few words about that scene, and then repeating the process while going deeper into your visioning process. Right now, can you imagine feeling those feelings that you fear so much, and being able to handle the experience successfully? If not, name the objections, and imagine that you have overcome these objections. Once you find a possible

yes, imagine what you would do to navigate these feelings. Would you writhe on the floor in pain? Would you yell and scream? Would you wail and cry? Imagine going all the way through this experience, in a way that feels emotionally honest to you. What would your experience have been like? Imagine yourself feeling every last little bit of these feared feelings. Imagine being on the other side of this long-feared experience, having washed yourself of it all—in a new state of emotional and spiritual hygiene. Then imagine how much more openly and realistically you could deal with your life. How would you then be different? (Some physical expression of your feelings may be helpful when doing this exercise, such as hitting a pile of pillows and yelling, while situated in a safe and private place.)

13

Being Willing Not to Know
How Things Will Turn Out

Affirmation:

I SENSE THAT a change is required, but I don't know exactly how this change will be accomplished, who will help me, or what the end result will look like. I will patiently wait, and pay attention to the way that life speaks to me, so that God can reveal how this change will unfold.

Core Idea:

It is a function of the ego to think that it has all the answers. The ego—that part of our conscious self that runs the show called our life—wants to remain in the central position of importance, and in an effort to do this, it tells us that it has all the answers. We need to realize that this is a trick, a way for the ego to remain in power. It is also a way that we avoid surrendering to what God has in mind for us, or said differently, it is a way we avoid surrendering to our life's transformative purpose.

The ego blocks this natural movement toward inner growth, and desperately holds onto its present state. The ego fears that by surrendering, by releasing its tight holding, it will be annihilated, will dissolve, and will cease to exist. It is paradoxical that humans so intently protect and try to maintain this blocked and limited state of consciousness. It is ironic because this holding on creates more fear and suffering. Only through the release of this tight holding-on can we reach a new and more expanded consciousness, a new place where we can then create new and better life circumstances.

Part of the problem is that we humans believe that we are our egos. We identify with the brain, with the mind, and we ignore the fact that we are much more than that. We cannot experience ourselves as the God-connected beings that we truly are as long as we think we are only our egos, as long as the ego insists on running the show of our life, and as long as our ego insists that only it knows what is best for us. So long as we permit the ego to keep holding on, we will be blocked from fluidly moving with God's will, and agilely changing to fit the truth of the new circumstances.

The ego is only a fragment of who we are. Part of why we are on earth is to expand our consciousness, to enlarge our understanding of, and experience of, who we really are. We are here on earth to reclaim and integrate those parts of us from which we are estranged. When we accomplish this integration, we expand our field of operation, that is to say that new possibilities open up.

As a starting place, we need to express our intention to go beyond our separated and limited state of consciousness, and we need to pray for assistance with these efforts. This wider view must be fought for, and it will take considerable effort. The ego will make it appear as though maintaining the status quo is the safe and easy path of least resistance. But following the ego's advice will only lead to more stagnation, further pain, and expanded suffering.

In an effort to hold on to the status quo, in which the ego runs our lives, the ego will engage in a variety of tricks, or con games, ways that it talks us into not changing. If we fall for these tricks, we maintain our separated and limited state.

To facilitate change, we must notice how the ego is causing us to stiffen up against change. We need to notice how the ego is making maintaining the status quo look more desirable than being open, flexible, and moving with the truth. For example, the ego may say it will be humiliating or embarrassing to change, and that the personality cannot suffer such a fate. Likewise, the ego may make the proposed new state appear to be life threatening, appear to be unbearable, and/or appear to be much worse than it actually is.

Underlying these and many other possible tricks is the ego's prideful claim that it really does know the truth about the nature of consciousness, and it really does know what's best for a particular person. Since the ego is only a separated part of who we really are, it cannot know these things. To break this stranglehold of the ego, notice how the ego uses fear and distrust to keep us in an unmoving and stagnant state, how it uses these things to block the change that we consciously say we want. After we identify these ego tricks, we gain the opportunity to challenge them, and only in the challenge and the comparison to the truth can we clearly see that the tricks do not serve us, and that they only keep us stuck. Then we can make a grounded choice to change for the better.

Personal Story:

Mandy had just retired from twenty-five years of service with the electric company, and she really wanted to give back to her church, an organization that she had received so much from over the years. She was struck that there were no volunteers at the church when it came to administrative matters, although many other types of volunteering were in evidence. She decided that she would try and make a difference in this area. After a few conversations with members of the Board of Directors, she proposed and received the go-ahead to prepare a guidebook for administrative volunteers.

Virtually all the administrative work at this particular church was currently done by a full-time employee called Zelda. This woman was cold, aloof, remote, and emotionally unavailable. The lack of volunteering in the administrative area probably had something to do with the way Zelda acted, the way she believed she owned all things in the administrative area. Mandy's efforts to prepare a guidebook for volunteers ran up against Zelda's resistance. For example, Zelda blamed Mandy, saying Mandy had not done sufficient research about the administrative procedures at the church, and Zelda used that alleged problem as an excuse to claim Mandy didn't know what she was talking about, to stonewall, and to otherwise continue to be uncooperative.

Mandy's consequential reaction to Zelda involved a lot of self-blame and self-accusation. Just as she had repeatedly done when she was a child, Mandy went to this inner place of believing there must be something the matter with her. She repeatedly tried to engage Zelda in conversations about how volunteers could help at the church, but Zelda refused to deal with Mandy, insisting that she funnel all conversations through an email-based contact management program, instead of simply dealing with Mandy on the phone or in person. Mandy used this refusal to interact as a further reason to beat herself up, to believe she had failed at her task with the church.

Soon thereafter, in a conversation with her long-time friend Sven, Mandy realized that she had given up on Zelda. Mandy believed that Zelda just wasn't interested in having volunteers help her. Sven assisted Mandy in appreciating that perhaps Zelda was just feeling threatened, like her job was in some way in jeopardy. Sven also helped Mandy to consider that just because Zelda wasn't interested in, or supportive of, what Mandy was doing today, didn't mean that Zelda would always be that way. Mandy then saw that by treating Zelda as an obstacle, as an obstruction to getting the job done, Mandy was making things worse. For example, Mandy's complaints to the Board about Zelda's lack of cooperation only caused Zelda to be still more defensive, uncommunicative, and emotionally unavailable.

Sven helped Mandy to see that her job, at least at this point in time, was not to prepare a volunteer guidebook. It was instead to generate a conversation amongst the leaders in the church, a conversation in which each of the participants in church leadership activities asked God to help them to see whether they were giving their very best, for the sake of the community, for the sake of God, and if not, in what ways they were not. Mandy embraced the generation of that new conversation, and the propagation of that conversation across the church hierarchy, as her new volunteer job.

As a result of that conversation, a number of important changes took place at the church. For example, the board of directors adopted a formal set of job descriptions for leaders within the church, even though this change had—up until this point in time—been actively resisted by Zelda. It was Mandy's willingness to embrace the possibility that she didn't really know what was going on, that shifted things for her. Being open to God speaking to her, through her friend Sven, facilitated her efforts to make a contribution to the church. After that new conversation about "giving your best" was absorbed by the church hierarchy, the volunteer guidebook could then be prepared by Mandy in a straightforward and businesslike manner.

Journal Questions:

(1) If you are using an ego trick (which could be simply redefined as an imagined story that blocks transcendence of the separated ego self) to keep yourself from changing, what exactly is this ego trick? Maybe you are saying you don't want to be gullible because, after all, this transformation process hasn't yet been widely endorsed by authority figures? Perhaps you flatter yourself by saying that having doubts about this transformation process is somehow intelligent or prudent? Or perhaps you employ an excuse like "I haven't yet gathered enough information in order to make a good decision about next steps"? Or maybe you say something to yourself such as "I am too worried and apprehensive to relax enough to let go of the ego"? Or perhaps your ego claims that you aren't intelligent enough to do the complex inner work that seems to be necessary in order to deal with all the many things going on inside of you? If you use any of these or other

ego tricks, are these claims of the ego true? Or are you using these claims of the ego as rationalizations to dodge the fact that you are simply scared?

(2) Are you willing to loosen up the way that you look at the change you contemplate such that you bring a "maybe" to the process? Are you willing to get out of a dualistic "yes" or "no" about the change process? If you currently have a "no" about this process, or if you are not open to the possibility that you don't yet have all the answers about how the change will proceed, then how is it that you are going to allow God to inspire you?

(3) If you look at your life in broad sweeping terms, you can probably come up with a bunch of examples where you undertook a big project, or made a serious life-changing decision, and you didn't know how it would turn out. You may have taken a new job, or moved to a different city, or married somebody, without knowing how it would turn out. Why is it that this new change that you contemplate should be any different?

14

Calling Yourself on the Tricks You Play

Affirmation:

I AM MORE than my ego consciousness; I have vast resources of truth, wisdom, and perspective on which I can draw. I choose now to open to and be connected to this vaster self. I ask this place deep within myself to inform me how I have been deceiving myself, and how I have been tricking myself into believing that I can't make a change.

Core Idea:

Everybody has an ego, that part of us which is the traffic cop that runs their life, the volitional thinking part of them, the will faculty that runs their life. The ego can memorize, learn, and collect information. It can repeat information it has gathered from other sources, and it can follow in the footsteps of other people. It is equipped to remember, sort, and select information. It can make decisions, both out in the world and in terms of how to run one's inner world. But it is not creative. It cannot deeply experience feelings, such as pleasure. The ego cannot deeply know the truth either. Egos are important, and they are needed in order to run our day-to-day lives. We use our egos for instance when driving, as we decide to proceed at the same speed through an intersection because the traffic light is green, or to speed up or come to a stop because the light has turned yellow.

The ego is separated from the real self—that is to say it is separated from our innermost self. The real self is connected to God, to others, and to All-That-Is. The real self is Creation itself and all that Creation includes, such as nature. When we are connected to the real self we have a constructive, joyous, and creative experience. All that is beautiful, great, generous, and life enhancing comes from the real self. Likewise, wisdom and a sense of the true meaning of life come only from the real self. If we suffer from recurring episodes in which we feel like life is meaningless, this is a tip-off that we are separated from our real selves.

It is important to have an adequately strong ego in order to properly deal with life. For example, we must stick up for ourselves and set proper boundaries, and having an adequately strong and well-developed ego is required in order to do this successfully. Too weak an ego would allow others to abuse and manipulate us. While a strong ego is important, having too strong an ego is a hindrance to connecting with the real self. Too strong an ego holds on tenaciously, and refuses to give over to the real self.

So a balance is required if the ego is to work harmoniously with the real self. The task of the ego, with respect to the real self, is to run a life and take care of what needs to be taken care of, and also to create the personal habits and spiritual practices which then allow the real self to manifest. For example, a balanced but adequately strong ego would make enough money so that an individual could have some unscheduled time to meditate. A balanced and adequately strong ego would then make the time to meditate, in order to invite the real self to come through into the forefront of our consciousness.

So a healthy ego is one that is strong, but not overly strong, and acts in cooperation with the real self. An overly strong ego thinks that it is all that a person is, and it denies, blocks, or otherwise obstructs the real self. Holding on to the ego too tightly, and not working harmoniously with the real self, is a function of fear. The specific fear that may be coming up could be the fear of life, of feelings, of pleasure, of other people, and/or maybe of everything. In this respect, holding on to the ego leads to withdrawal from living, hiding from life, and a refusal to engage fully with all that life has to offer.

To move into a joyous and empowered experience of life, where one is evolving and making necessary changes, the ego needs to relax, and also call upon the real self for help. The ego, when acting alone, is in fact unable to successfully deal with life. The ego requires the powers of the real self to complement it, so that together with the real self it may successfully deal with all that life requires and provides. The ego is thus just part of the full consciousness, a relatively small part of the available consciousness, that can be brought to bear on the problems, issues, tasks, pleasures, and other aspects of life.

The ego is run by fear, as long as it operates on a limited level of understanding. In other words, the ego's fears about its inability to deal with life are justified, as long as it refuses to take advantage of the wisdom, the truth, the power, and the deep feelings of the real self. Thus, to come out of a painful and repetitive situation, where we aren't able to move to the next level of personal evolution, we must call upon the creativity and understanding that only the real self possesses. It is the role of the ego to call in those parts of the real self, and then to temporarily step aside so that the real self can manifest.

Personal Story:

A young woman in her early twenties, Connie was accustomed to putting other people's desires above her own. She was endlessly trying to curry favor with others. She would do this by being helpful, by providing unsolicited information to people whom she thought could benefit from it, by doing unnecessary favors for others, and by taking on projects for which she didn't have the time or resources. All of these strategies were unconsciously intended to cause other people to like her, and were intended to help insure that she would be protected in the future, because these same people would then supposedly be there for her. She wasn't comfortable with this type of engagement with other people, because on some level she felt like she was a doormat that people walked all over. On another level, she was uncomfortable with this type of behavior because it felt artificial and contrived, like some game in which she did things for other people so they would owe her something in the future.

Connie grew up in a physically violent family, where her father would hit her and yell, sometimes so intensely and forcefully that she would faint, thinking that she must be dead this time. Her father's unpredictable and uncontrollable rage served to alienate all of Connie's extended family, who didn't dare to come anywhere near the household, lest they become the next target for her father's rage. Connie's mother was totally subservient to, intimidated by, and dominated by Connie's father. At the same time, because nobody else was around the house, except her weak-willed younger brother, who was certainly not going to stand up to her father, Connie's only hope for protection was her mother. Connie's mother was emotionally unavailable, but Connie decided, at a very young age, that she must somehow please her mother. Gaining her mother's favor was the only strategy that could conceivably assure her safety.

As a result of this pseudo-solution to life ("pseudo" is used here because this approach really doesn't work; only the child inside us thinks such strategies will work), Connie became accustomed to paying close attention to others' desires and preferences, which she proceeded to make far more important than her own. Needless to say, she was overwhelmed by all the projects, tasks, and personal favors that she performed for others. Her life seemed to be a mad scramble to satisfy all the many people in her life. The way that others took advantage of Connie's approach to life just made things worse, because they often abused her by asking for still more "favors." And Connie would agree, thinking that she must do these things, in order to hopefully be protected by these people at some point in the future. This behavior was compulsive and caused a variety of problems. For example, it would cause Connie to neglect the basic requirements of her job, and this in turn provoked periodic run-ins with her boss.

Connie was operating with a fundamental misunderstanding about life. Using her child consciousness, she enlisted her ego to follow this pseudo-solution to life, believing that if she didn't get others' support and favor, then she would surely die. While that may have felt true for a small child, when she was totally dependent on her mother for protection against her violent father, it was not true for an adult woman who was living on her own, an adult woman who had no violent people around her.

Connie came to this insight through her meditations and psychology readings. In meditation, a voice deep within her spoke to her, revealing how she had been blunting the possibility that life offered, how she had been holding her real self back, and how she had been creating her own unhappiness. Believing she needed help, she joined a support group for those with similar issues.

Through intimate conversations in that that small group, she came to see that her preoccupation with pleasing others had been a way to hide from her own life. She saw how the frantic attempts to please everyone were in fact leaving her with no time to take care of herself, let alone time to sense and honor her own true needs. She also saw how her exclusive focus on the needs of others had blocked her ability to relax and have pleasure, and that too interfered with the manifestation of her real self.

Through her work in the small group, she additionally noticed that when her pseudo-solution wasn't working, she would just try harder, and that of course consumed still more of her scarce time. She appreciated how she was stuck in an unworkable vicious circle. Through the aid of the voice of her real self, she understood how her pseudo-solution in fact could never work, because it was based on a false assumption about life (that she must be protected by others in order to survive).

Connie eventually saw how she had a weak ego in one area of her psyche: she had given up her power to say "no" to the many requests made by others. She also saw that she had too strong an ego in another area of her psyche: she had doggedly and tenaciously maintained the same pseudo-solution, insisting that it was going to be her salvation, her recipe for success in life. By spending more time in quiet meditation, and asking for more information about her situation, she continued to get insights about how she might make constructive changes. These realizations helped her dramatically change the way she engaged with life, and the way she approached interactions with other people. These realizations also allowed her to come to a deeper sense of the spiritual meaning of her life, and what she had come to earth to learn.

Journal Questions:

(1) As discussed in the prior chapter, ego tricks are maneuvers that the ego uses to keep from opening to the real self, they are the way in which the ego stays separate. For example, one ego trick involves being very busy, preventing oneself from taking the time to really honestly assess what's going on, and thus preventing oneself from dropping into a relaxed place where the real self could come through into the foreground of consciousness. That ego trick will successfully block the available inspiration and wisdom from coming through. What ego trick, or ego tricks, do you utilize in order to keep the real self in the background of your consciousness? Be specific about what you do and how it works.

(2) If the real self is not manifesting in the forefront of your consciousness, it will be very difficult for you to

consciously acknowledge the all-encompassing-truth of your situation. What collateral damage, what side effects, are you creating in your life because you keep avoiding the confrontation with this truth that you now need to have? Write about how you hurt both yourself and others because you create this collateral damage and these side effects.

(3) The ego creates false battles, battles that don't need to be fought, in order to maintain its place of dominance and control over your consciousness. For example, consider that the ego maintains a misconception that it has to fight to maintain its present state of consciousness, or else it will be overwhelmed by and destroyed by the real self. Entertain the possibility that the real self does not want to dominate, overwhelm, or destroy the ego; it only seeks to merge with, to connect with, and harmoniously work with the ego. In a quiet few moments of relaxation, constructively use the ego to request guidance, inspiration, and insight from the real self, and then be open to genuinely engaging with whatever comes forward.

15

Stopping Impulsive and Unthinking Behaviors

Affirmation:

I CALL ON my higher self to help me to understand the long-term implications of my actions. In particular, please show me where I have been acting blindly, impulsively, and in an unthinking manner. I genuinely want to bring more awareness to these behaviors. No matter what they may look like, please help me to see the motivations for, and the consequences of, these behaviors.

Core Idea:

To contextualize the investigation into those places where we need to do more personal work, consider that there are four broadly defined stages of evolution into which each aspect of our psyches can be placed. Seeing where we stand in a certain area within our own psyches will help us to zero-in on what is causing our pain, on what is blocking our progress, and on what is causing certain undesirable situations to be perpetuated in our lives. In those areas of our psyche in which we have been wounded and where we still have unresolved pain, there we are most often the least evolved. It is in these specific areas that we need to some additional personal work. It is into those areas that we need to bring a new consciousness, so that these aspects can then grow up and be on par with the other aspects of our being.

At the lowest level of evolution are those places where we respond with automatic reflexes, where we respond blindly and impulsively. On this first and least-evolved level of consciousness, when we have an emotional reaction, we fly into an upset. At such a point in time, we are just responding according to deeply imprinted wrong ideas about life. These ideas are most often generalizations that perhaps were true when we were children, but which as adults are no longer true. These generalizations about life can be called "images," because they fix some aspect of life as though it never moves, as though it never evolves.

When we respond with an emotional reaction, we are blind, and don't see the big picture. The part that is responding with an emotional reaction is our child self, our lower self. Our lower self is often embarrassed about the consequences of our impulsively acting out. In an attempt to make things right, the lower self will typically don a mask to try to cover up or justify what caused these episodes of acting out (episodes could involve yelling, hitting, or insulting others, or a wide variety of other destructive behaviors). The mask may, for example, attempt to rationalize these destructive behaviors, with words like "You forced me to defend myself," or "I did that because my parents screwed-me-up." These mask cover-ups are never convincing, but when we use them, they nonetheless do reveal that we have lower-self aspects about which we have embarrassment, shame, and/or guilt.

Acting impulsively, blindly, automatically, is the result of lower-self material that we have been unwilling to face. Where we feel enslaved, and where we don't feel free – those are the areas in which we act impulsively, blindly, and automatically. This behavior is always destructive. It blocks love, and it cripples our creativity. It prevents us from responding to the truth of a particular situation. In these moments we are always living in the past.

To overcome this impulsivity, these fixed places, we must move into the second of the four stages of evolution that were mentioned above. This next stage up the evolutionary ladder involves awareness, a place where we notice that we are doing something that is destructive, something that doesn't work, or something that causes pain for ourselves and/or for others. In this stage, we give up our explanations, our justifications, and our excuses, about why we repeatedly act in blind and impulsive ways. In this second stage, we give up the self-deception and the denial that reinforce the impulsive and blind behaviors. The transition to the second stage (awareness) is difficult because we must admit that we have been driven by superstitions, unreasonable fears, over-generalizations, and no-longer-relevant responses to life.

To move to the second stage of evolution we must note our vanity, our pride, and our commitment to looking good. We must admit that, at least in this one aspect of our psyche, we are not quite as evolved as we thought we were (or told others that we were). When we acknowledge, accept, and allow these lower-self aspects, i.e., the ones that would hold us still longer in blindness, in this prison of automatic and impulsive behavior, then we can look at what's happening with a more objective stance. This in turn allows us to choose to no longer be blindly driven by our lower self, and to evolve ourselves in this one very painful area of our lives.

Note that it is our higher self (also called our real self) that assists in the movement from the first to the second stage of evolution. Our higher self sees the big picture; our higher self allows us to see both cause and effect; our higher self offers up a preferable way to be, a way that is no longer blindly driven by the lower self. It is our higher self that can choose to modify our behaviors, and it is our higher self that can keep us on the path of no longer being a victim to our lower self. It is the higher self that can act as a parent by using constructive discipline, and by no longer allowing the childish lower self to dictate how we will act.

The third stage of personal evolution involves understanding. This understanding brings an appreciation of why this behavior exists, how it was created, and when it will most likely be provoked again in the future. It involves an appreciation of how the original painful situation in one's past is like, or perhaps not like, the present situation. This understanding also involves an appreciation of why this blind impulsive reactivity is no longer appropriate. The third stage furthermore involves understanding the misconceptions and false assumptions that we have made about life, that have in turn prompted us to behave in ways that do not serve others nor do they serve ourselves.

The fourth and highest stage of human personal evolution involves knowing the truth. In this stage, we deeply feel the truth about what it is that we have been doing, and why it is that we have employed this behavior to deal with the world. For example, in this stage, we feel remorse about the damage and destruction that we have created, and for the ways that we have hurt other people. Here we see both our errors and the deeper truth. This is not an intellectual experience; it is instead a spiritual embracing of the truth. Deep inside ourselves, when we are in this stage, we understand the laws of the universe and how they apply to us. When we inhabit this stage, we exert a healing effect on both ourselves and on others. In this stage will bring both balance and order into our lives, because we will be living in a manner compatible with the truth.

Personal Story:

Brian was a night owl, often staying up until midnight. His girlfriend, Sherry, was an early-to-bed and early-to-rise woman, in part because she was a nurse and her shift often began early in the morning. One evening when he was staying over at her house, he was kissing her goodnight at nine o'clock as he was tucking her into bed. She then said, "How long are you going to be?" This question threw him into an emotional reaction. He felt the anger bubbling up inside, and he knew there would be hell to pay if he allowed his authentic reaction to come out the way his lower self wanted it to come out. His lower self wanted to say, "What the hell does it matter—you aren't going to know if I'm here or not—you're going to be asleep." Instead he simply responded with the dutiful words, "Not long, dear."

As he walked into the living room after this incident he asked himself, "Why was that so upsetting to me?" Brian's emotional reaction seemed all out of proportion to the circumstances. He asked for guidance to know what was happening within him, and then started writing some ideas down. All sorts of things came forward in answer to that question.

Brian saw how he repeatedly and automatically contorted himself into strange emotional shapes in order to please Sherry. He tried to please her dutifully because he knew that she was always looking for some evidence that he genuinely loved her. It was as if he was the ocean, and he had to always be bringing the tide in. But neither the ocean nor intimate relationships are like that. In both, the tide comes in some-times, the tide goes out sometimes, and sometimes it does neither (it's just static). Brian saw how artificial it was to al-ways keep trying to please Sherry, to always keep reassuring her that he loved her, to always keep her from being upset about him not loving her enough.

Sitting in the living room, he realized how furious he was about the way his relationship with Sherry had been taking place. He seethed and raged on paper, writing about how he felt as though he had entirely given up what he wanted to do, in the interests of making sure that Sherry was happy. He came to appreciate how he had made her the equivalent of his mother. He came from a single-parent family, and his mother was suicidal and often depressed. He was often the one whom his mother designated as the court jester, the one to cheer her up, the one to make her feel as though life was worth living. Meanwhile, Brian was always worried that if he didn't achieve this elusive goal, then his mother would com-mit suicide, and he would thus become an orphan.

Brian saw how he had used all sorts of mask justifications to support his continued compulsive pleasing of women. He would tell others that pleasing women is the man's job, and that he must, according to gender roles, take care of women. He would tell others that men didn't get to pursue their own goals, that they had to be there so as to support women in their pursuit of family goals. He would tell himself that he was selfish if he actually stood up for himself, or if he actually asserted his own desires and needs. But all of these explanations and justifications were smoke screens, and none of them rang true for him. They were all just mechanisms he used to keep from looking at how he was transferring his painful experience with his mother onto his girlfriend.

In this place of seeing clearly how he had been acting toward Sherry, he felt a bit disoriented, seasick, unstable, and ungrounded. But this was simply the temporary experience of getting used to a new plateau in his own personal evolution. He vowed then and there to stop making himself a slave to women, and to stop catering to women's requests so blindly and impulsively. He saw clearly that Sherry was not his mother. He saw how he had given away his adult power to Sherry, even though she had never asked for that. He saw how this type of engagement with wives and girlfriends had made him emotionally dependent, the way he had been dependent on his mother.

Brian soon thereafter requested that Sherry join him in an experiment that was intended to bring more of these understandings to the forefront of Brian's consciousness. Brian asked, and Sherry agreed, for the next three months, to spend time together only if they both wanted to do so. In this type of experimental relationship, they would not call, text, email or in any other way communicate with the other if they didn't really feel like it. The couple wouldn't do things, or go places, or otherwise be together, unless both parties genuinely wanted to do so. Both parties would openly share about their needs and desires, and neither would act as though they were sacrificing for the other. As a result of the experiment, the couple grew much closer because they communicated about new things which had had, up until that point in time, been held back.

Journal Questions:

(1) What blind, impulsive, and unthinking behaviors do you engage in, and then later regret? Make a list including at least five of these behaviors. Identify the one behavior on this list that creates the greatest pain and trouble in your life, and put an asterisk next to it.

(2) With what reasons do you justify this most painful and troubling behavior? Make a complete list. Then honestly determine whether you find these reasons truly compelling and convincing. You can put a "Y" (Yes) or an "N" (No) next to each reason.

(3) Again looking at this most painful and troublesome behavior, what intention is in evidence? Do you really and genuinely want to create positively in the world? Pause for a moment and feel into the question before you provide an answer. Allow the answer to come forward as an organic and deeply felt manifestation, rather than showing up as simply an intellectual response. If you don't

genuinely feel this desire for the positive, this intention to create positively in the world, why not? If you have self-consciousness about answering this question with anything but a resounding "yes," set that self-consciousness aside for this exercise.

16

Acknowledging the Existence of Negative Desires

Affirmation:

I ASK FOR divine assistance—may I be shown the unconscious and concealed negative desires that block me from making the positive changes that I seek.

Core Idea:

If we feel blocked when it comes to making a desired positive change in our lives, we must in some way be saying "no" to this desired change. Our life circumstances provide us with immediate feedback, illuminating the law of cause and effect. If we have not yet accomplished the change we seek, then on some level we don't want to make that change. For many of us, a negative desire, a wish not to change, is unconscious. Unconscious desires are more influential than, and will win out over, conscious desires. The way to change this state of affairs is to make the unconscious negative desire a conscious negative desire. Only when it is made conscious can this desire be challenged, and later modified, or in some cases simply dropped.

In order to reach a state of inner alignment, a state of inner unity, which then will allow the desired change to proceed, we must all take responsibility for what we have created in our lives. If, for example, we are suffering because a particular relationship is disharmonious, we have a choice about how we are going to deal with it. We can blame and complain, we can feel sorry for ourselves, and/or we can feel like a victim. Or we can start to see that we have contributed to this disharmonious relationship via our words, our actions, our feelings, and our thoughts. When we take responsibility for our contribution, then we can start to change things. Without this self-responsibility, we are simply blind and stumbling along in our suffering.

When we open to being responsible for our life experiences, for our life creations, we start to appreciate that suffering is ultimately unnecessary. It is true that we must accept what we have created, but this is only a temporary manifestation of our inner errors, misconceptions, and problems. If we take the reins of the horse called our life, if we guide it and direct it, then temporary suffering is simply a tip-off that there is some inner work to do. This temporary suffering is in fact a gift from the spirit world, a red flag directing us to what needs attention.

To come out of this unnecessary suffering, we must accept all the consequences of our ignorance and errors. We must also embrace the concept that we are free creatures, that we have free will. We must genuinely want to change, and we must channel this genuine desire for change into a willingness to both accept and confront our negative desires. We must fully be with what is true right now, especially the consequences of our negative desires. The longer we resist and deny our current situation, the longer we look away from our negative desires, the longer the pain and suffering will continue.

Inhabiting this transformative place of being reconciled to the present temporary existence of our negative desires, of allowing ourselves to go into related feelings, thoughts, pain and suffering, will bring us to a place of nonresistance, a place of allowing. This is not to say that we want to stay in this difficult place, but we must fully experience, and go through this reality, in order to move to the next level. We cannot skip steps. Thus, paradoxically, we must accept, be with, and go to that place that we so ardently and strenuously resist, in order to free ourselves from our self-created prisons.

This place of deeply accepting and embracing the present truth is known by many of the people suffering with serious and terminal diseases. They have found that if they hold this pain and suffering softly, if they embrace it on all levels of their being, the pain then changes in nature. Then the pain becomes something fluid and malleable. In fact, their condition is then no longer painful. But if they resist the pain, if they struggle against it, then they perpetuate and even accentuate the pain. This is the difference between soft pain and hard pain. Soft pain can and does change, but hard pain is simply reinforced and maintained.

If we can embrace our negative wishes, or negative desires, in this place of soft pain, in this place of acceptance, self-responsibility, and strict and utter truth, then we can start to evolve these same negative wishes. We must feel and be with the part that wishes to hold onto these negative desires. We must investigate the origins and causative factors behind them. We can bring understanding and support to this place that we have pushed away, this place that we have ostracized from our consciousness, when we can befriend and nurture this place. In this open and inwardly flexible place, we often find that the negative desires organically begin to change. Like those who have discovered the power of the soft pain approach, in the process of understanding, supporting, and being with it—it is here that the negative place can and does evolve.

Pain and suffering is always the result of having an inner split, a place where we are pulled in two (or perhaps more) contradictory directions. The negative desire is not a permanent manifestation; it is only a temporary part of us that needs to evolve. Embracing it and getting to know it does not mean that it is all of us, or even the real nature of who we ultimately are. Embracing this place in a spirit of truth does not mean that we will perpetuate it. The willingness to go through this process will later bring us out of feelings of being a helpless victim. Instead, it will bring us back to knowing ourselves as free, autonomous, and self-responsible.

Personal Story:

Mitch had a childhood that many would say was blessed and fortunate. He came from a long-standing and reputable family in his town, and he went to good schools. His family had money, and his basic needs were well taken care of. When Mitch was forty-five years old, it was, in light of all these advantages, distressing to both him and his family that he was not able to maintain a long-term relationship with a woman. In spite of the fact that he was heterosexual, Mitch lost interest in every woman he had dated at about the time—when the woman decided she wanted to be with him in a long-term relationship.

It was almost as if dating was a game, and Mitch's objective was to get the woman to open up to him emotionally, to decide that she wanted him to be her partner. When she did so, the relationship no longer held any magnetic attraction for Mitch, and he was gone. One evening, over a couple of beers, in a conversation with one of his longtime buddies, Mitch talked about his pattern, and how painful it was, because consciously Mitch did want to have a long-term partner and a wife.

His buddy, Crawford, asked him why he didn't want a part-ner. Mitch was at first annoyed and taken aback by the ques-tion. He asked Crawford why he was posing such a question. Mitch then got defensive, and at first wouldn't even admit that he might have a negative desire, a desire not to be married. In response Crawford said, "Based on the results in your life, part of you must not want to get married."

It was only later that weekend that Mitch was willing to once again talk about this topic with Crawford. Mitch shared how the experience of marriage was for his mother and father. His mother was extremely dominating and controlling, and she told Mitch's father exactly what to do all the time. Mitch lost respect for his father, considering him to be a wimp and a milquetoast. In spite of this judgment about his father, to a large extent Mitch remained a man controlled by his mother. It was not surprising for Crawford to hear how Mitch felt great relief when he moved out of his parents' house as soon as he turned eighteen years old. Mitch loved the freedom and self-direction that bachelorhood provided. He admitted that there was a part of him that was afraid that if he married, he would become like his father, that he would be dominated, controlled, henpecked, and nagged.

Crawford challenged the belief that Mitch held, a belief that marriage must turn out to be the same as it was for his parents. Crawford invited Mitch to find a different kind of woman, one who gave him space to be himself, who encouraged him to have his own life, a woman who didn't want to dominate and control him. Mitch thought this was a grand idea, especially because he had consistently been attracting and dating women who showed many of the same traits that his mother had.

Mitch met a beautiful woman named Cindy soon thereafter. Cindy was depressed and going through her own stuff, with the help of a prescription antidepressant drug. This wasn't exactly what Mitch had in mind, but her depression turned out to give him lots of space to have his own life, to be himself, and to experiment with a new concept about intimate relationships. Over the course of several months, as Cindy gradually got over her depression, she showed up more and more, and Mitch came to appreciate that she not only loved him, and supported him, but that she had no intention of dominating and controlling him. Cindy later got off her medication, and Mitch was relieved to see that even then she still didn't want to dominate and control him. Seventeen years later, Mitch is still happily married to Cindy.

Journal Questions:

(1) Even if you've done this exercise before, make a comprehensive list of all the reasons why you want the sought-after change in your life, and be sure to be specific. Then make a list of all of the reasons why you don't want this same change, and again be specific. Then cross out any of these reasons, on either list, that are out of touch with

reality. After that, cross out the remaining reasons that are honestly inconsequential and/or irrelevant. Next, cross out those remaining reasons that really don't serve both you and others. Then check in with yourself, and ask whether you feel differently about the important change that you seek.

(2) Explain why certain reasons in favor of a change are at odds with reasons against the change. Where is the point of conflict? Are there other options you had not yet seriously considered, places where these conflicting intentions are not in conflict? Go through each of the conflicts, asking God to reveal a new unified place where no conflict exists.

(3) Name a situation in which you could have made a significant, positive step forward, in the direction of making the change that you say you desire, but then you faltered. What thoughts were you thinking at that moment? What feelings did you have then? Be specific because it is in these specifics that a new empowered perspective can grow.

17

Viewing Your Dysfunctional Pseudo-Solutions

Affirmation:

I ASK FOR divine assistance so that I may clearly see the destructive and dysfunctional ways that I have been dealing with life. I also ask that I be shown a different and more constructive way to be, a way aligned with my deep inner truth.

Core Idea:

Our deeper selves know what's right for us. In that place, when we connect to it—perhaps in meditation or prayer—there is no uncertainty, there are no doubts, and there is no wavering. In that deep inner truth, we have a sense that a particular course of action is right. In that place, we allow our deeper intuitive nature to guide us, because here we trust our own truth.

In order to access this place, we must clear away our misconceptions about life and past events, and also clear away our dysfunctional ways of dealing with life (the latter can be referred to as "pseudo-solutions"). These things have collectively blocked us from accessing our deeper truth, which can be likened to the sun that is obscured by clouds on a cloudy day. Like the sun, our deeper truth is always there, even though it may not be visible in this moment. Rather than being far away, our deeper truth is readily accessible if we open to that possibility, if we lay the groundwork for that connection to the deeper truth to happen.

There is nothing to fear about this deeper truth, this place where our real self abides. This deeper truth is not strange or a mystery. We have all connected with it in the past. Nonetheless, we prefer to dwell on our outer selves. That is to say, we have become accustomed to operating with our misconceptions about life, our misinterpretations of past events, and our pseudo-solutions. Our distracting outer self includes our compulsive drives, such as the belief that we must experience a certain scenario in life, otherwise we cannot be happy. With this erroneous belief, when our will is not done, when these scenarios are not experienced, then on an emotional level we feel as though all is lost.

To make sure that our will is done, based on our misconceptions about life and our misinterpretations about past events, we adopt certain strategies, certain pseudo-solutions. One example of a pseudo-solution is: "I must be cruel and pushy, otherwise I will never get my way with other people." This pseudo-solution may have been adopted after a child was ignored for many years by his or her parents. With her limited outlook on life, the child may have determined that acting in this manner was one successful way to get attention (any type of attention, even punishment, may have been better than being ignored).

To clear away these metaphorical clouds, to open to the opportunity to make contact with our deeper truth, we need to feel all our feelings about having our will frustrated. We need to understand how these feelings drive us to behave compulsively, drive us to adopt certain manipulative strategies to force both life and others to abide by our will. We need to feel just how important always getting our way has become, how it has become—on a feeling level—a matter of life and death. We can then begin to ask whether all this is indeed consistent with reality.

When we can make these thoughts and feelings conscious, we obtain a new power, and that power is about choosing another way to be. As long as these thoughts and feelings remain unconscious, we will continue to be enslaved and driven by them. With this new power of understanding, we can truthfully see that life, by its very nature, does not always give us all that we want. With this new power of understanding, we can also come to appreciate how our compulsive ways of behaving may actually be blocking us from manifesting the life scenarios that we yearn for. With this new understanding, we can calmly consider a new and more constructive way to be.

Personal Story:

Victor was an interesting and intelligent older man, as well as a very talented singer. Although employed at a local factory, he got great joy from his evenings spent at a local singing club. Outside of these two venues, he had only a handful of distant family friends with whom he occasionally stayed in touch. His life was otherwise quite lonely. Many people were turned off by his personal manner, which was bellicose, dictatorial, presumptuous, and tutorial in nature. He believed that the only way he could connect with others was if he told them what to do, if he taught them something. Needless to say, many people did not take kindly to this professorial "know-it-all" treatment.

It was the departure of a girlfriend that prompted him to reexamine the way he was conducting his relationships. He reflected on how his mother was dictatorial and cold, and how his mother was constantly telling people what to do. In his childhood experience, that way to behave seemed to convey a certain personal power, a certain ability to manifest things in the world. As a child, he had also been beaten up a good deal by bullies, and as a result he retreated into his studies, choosing to ignore sports and other physical pursuits (because his use of his body to get his way obviously wasn't working with the bullies). His many long hours spent studying later revealed that he knew things that some people did not, and this he thought was the key to making a contribution to them, and also the key to making a connection with them. The dictatorial and unempathetic ways of his mother, combined with his ideas about knowledge being the gift of what he had to offer, and his efforts to find some way to connect with others, all merged to form his current dysfunctional behavior regarding relationships.

Perhaps most painful of the recent events which brought his behavior to his attention was the way a family member had recently called him an "asshole," to his face, in front of many people, at large family dinner. This was a poignant and painful reflection of the fact that his personal way-of-being was not producing the sought-after results. In other words, his pseudo-solution wasn't working.

It was then that he admitted that he needed a different approach. At that point, he didn't know what that other approach might be, but he had become cracked open to a more heartfelt possibility. In this new and receptive space, he was open to others, and beginning to explore his conversations with them. He could now connect with them, share his feelings and emotions, and hear as well as receive theirs. In this place, he actually had several great conversations, conversations that were deeply personal and supportive to both parties. In this new cracked-open place, he chose to bring a new interpersonal flexibility, a new "let's see" attitude, to all his interactions. With this new choice he was surprised to find that he was able to create the loving connections that he had been yearning for, but due to his pseudo-solution, had not previously been able to create.

Journal Questions:

(1) What are the specific scenarios that you believe you absolutely must have in your life in order to be happy? For each one of these scenarios, identify why experiencing these situations is so important.

(2) When you don't manifest these scenarios, how does this make you feel? And in these moments, where your will is thwarted, what pseudo-solutions do you employ to force life and/or others to comply with your wishes? Consider that your pseudo-solutions are simply imagined ways to avoid the pain of not getting your way.

(3) In this same arena of your life, if you don't get your way, how do you behave with others? Are you pushy and demanding? Are you angry and do you yell? Perhaps you give people the silent-but-hurt treatment? Maybe you deny the situation entirely? What exactly is your own style in these moments? In these moments, how do you battle with the world, with your pain, and with all that you wish to avoid? Then, step back, look at this behavior objectively, and determine whether this behavior fosters or hinders the manifestation of your desired scenarios.

18

Overcoming Your Desire to Selfishly Act Out

Affirmation:

I CLEARLY SEE the negative and destructive consequences that are the result of acting out my lower self's selfish impulses. My higher self knows a better way to act, a way that is both positive and constructive. I choose now to align all of myself with my higher self, and to consistently come from that place.

Core Idea:

Most people suffered through childhoods in which they had to suppress their desires. Along with their legitimate needs, many also suppressed their selfish desires. This suppression often becomes unbearable and the lower self within us dictates certain behavior as a result. This is called "acting out," or more specifically, acting out of the lower self. In many cases, because these selfish desires have been suppressed, they fall into the unconscious, and this unconsciousness results in destructive acting out behavior, which inexplicably shows up from time to time.

Those who do not want to take responsibility for their actions may claim that they are helpless against these impulses to act out. But the truth is that every one of us can recognize and discern conduct that is selfish and damaging. Likewise, we can all step back and see the big picture, involving the long-term consequences of this acting out behavior. In the moment when we choose to see the big picture, we can decide to align ourselves with our higher selves. If we do that, we then behave in a different way, a way that is positive and constructive, in a way that considers others, not just ourselves.

Every one of us has the capacity to examine why we continue to behave in ways that are selfish and destructive. On some level, if we continue the behavior, we must believe that the behavior will be advantageous or pleasant for us. This may at first seem like a preposterous assertion. If we continue to act out in a way that is selfish and destructive, then there must be something inside us that believes it is best that we continue. To the extent that this something remains unconscious, we have no power over it. Instead, it rules us, causing us to behave in ways that are compulsive and not free. To the extent that this something is brought to the forefront of our conscious mind, to that extent can we question it, and determine whether it is in fact desirable and constructive to continue acting in this way.

Examining and challenging the idea that life causes us to act in these destructive and negative ways will often be the key to changing our behavior. This destructive idea about life is called an "image," because, like a photograph, it fixes some aspect of life (which by its very nature is continuously changing). When we take the time to illuminate the image, we reveal our confused and antiquated motives. For example, we may then discover that we have been acting in a way that we used to act, a way that is no longer reasonable and valid under the circumstances. We may look at life the way we did as a child, still thinking that we are helpless, when now we are in fact not helpless, nor are we any longer a child.

Instead of continuing with these destructive behavior patterns, we can call on our higher self to ask for assistance in gaining some objectivity and distance from our lower self, so that we can calmly step back and see what is happening. This observer perspective can help us notice the effects that are repeatedly created by the lower self when it acts out. Once we understand what it is that we have been doing, and why we have been doing those things, in addition to the destructive and negative consequences that this behavior creates, we can then be grounded in a choice to behave in a different way.

We don't need to deny our destructiveness, nor do we need to act it out in any way. We can express our feelings, our frustration, and/or our confusion, in ways that do not harm any person, and in ways that do not cause any damage to our position in the world. For instance, we can yell in the car while we drive alone on the highway, or we can beat a pillow when we are alone in our bedroom. We can know the irrational and destructive compulsions that we have, we can be fully aware of their presence within us, but can still act in a manner that is both positive and constructive. We do not need to be afraid of these feelings, these compulsions, or these impulses, because they are in their essence the same consciousness found in our higher self. These parts of our psyche are only naïve and wounded parts, operating with misconceptions and untruths; they are simply the child within us in need of some growing up.

In general, the lower self's belief in the need for selfishness comes from a belief in separation. If we instead embrace that all of us are connected, if we are all manifestations of God, then there is in reality no separation. From this place we see that selfishness is ultimately destructive, for both ourselves and for others. When we are coming from our higher selves, we can see a scenario where everyone benefits, where everyone's needs are met, where the needs of one are not opposed to the needs of another. Although at first this higher-self-inspired solution may seem nonexistent in the world, when we take a stand for such a solution, the way in which it could work then comes into view.

Personal Story:
Martha was a woman with deep feelings, a woman who loved to know, and be known by, many people. This great yearning

probably came from her emotionally desolate early childhood, where she was shown virtually no kindness or emotional warmth. She was primarily raised in a strict religious foster family, having been finally adopted out of the orphanage at the age of six. Before that she had been moved through a series of foster homes, occasionally back to live with her mother, who was a prostitute with severe problems with intravenous drugs. She never met her father, and did not know his identity, and so could not possibly live with him.

Martha's desire to know and be known was a great impetus for her to become a child psychiatrist. She was pleased that her training allowed her to work in the schools with poor kids, those who she thought needed the most support. This desire for intimate connection did not, however, show up in her love life. Although she was quite good-looking and dated frequently, she led a very lonely life. She was attracted to men with a lot of money, thinking that they were going to take care of her. But on another level of her psyche, she didn't dare allow anyone to take care of her, because she felt as though she had been so emotionally abandoned by both her biological and adoptive parents, and she was not going to allow that abandonment to happen again. On this physical and in-the-world level, she didn't trust that anyone would ever be there for her.

Having talked for many years with her girlfriends about having a family, it was difficult for Martha to admit that at forty-five, not only did she have no children, but she also didn't have a man who was seriously interested in getting married. It was the gap between what she said she wanted and what she actually had, and honestly confronting the truth about her biological clock running out, that caused her to investigate why she had created her life in this way.

Taking an objective inventory of her situation, she noticed that she wasn't really attracted to men who would make good fathers, or those who were interested in having a family. Instead, she was attracted to those who were workaholics, and who had a great deal of money, because she thought they would be able to take care of her. She was also intensely independent, and took pride in letting prospective lovers know that she didn't need them, in part because she hated the thought of being needy and dependent, as she had so painfully been when she was child. She furthermore saw that she had unconsciously been emotionally pushing away the men in her life, because she was afraid that they would break her heart, just the way that her heart had been broken repeatedly as a child.

Now that the possibility of her own biological family had come and gone, Martha changed her goals. She now simply wanted a boyfriend who could be her committed lover and spiritual partner. She had one former lover called Ben who was interested in starting something new with her, now that she had been changing the way she looked at intimate relationships. Ben was attracted to her in a new way, in part because Martha had stopped compulsively pushing him away in an effort to defend herself from the pain of a possible future broken heart. He was also encouraged because Martha was softening, instead of insisting on being hyper-independent. She now dwelt in the realization that everyone needed to love and be loved, and that everyone was interdependent. Ben thought her new approach to relationship afforded him a place where he might give to her, although he previously felt as though she was afraid to let him give to her. We left the story when Ben asked Martha to move in with him, although we don't know whether she took him up on the offer.

Journal Questions:

(1) In what way have you continued to act out in a manner that is both destructive and selfish? Be specific about what it is that you do. Then make a list of the negative and destructive consequences that come from this acting out.

(2) Specifically why do you believe that this acting out is an advisable behavior? Make a list of all the reasons why you think the behavior serves you, and/or why it is pleasurable.

(3) Name the erroneous image about the world on which the motives for your acting out are based. In other words, define the specific misconception about the world that forms the foundation for the motives, which, in turn, dictate that you continue to act out.

19

Having the Courage
to Be Yourself

Affirmation:

I AM A divine manifestation. The Creator uniquely expresses divine will through me. I pray that I may be a humble and worthy instrument for the expression of the Creator's will. I am on earth to do spiritual work, and I accept who and where I am today with respect to that work.

Core Idea:

Many people have a misconception about who they are relative to God. For example, they may believe that if they are truly self-responsible, then they choose to cut God out of their life. On the other hand, if God directs their life, then they will suffer, and they will have to put up with experiences they don't like. Those that step outside of this dualistic misconception may think that the alternative is atheism, but that too is a misconception.

We are, each one of us, connected to God. We are a part of God, extensions of God, as well as unique and artistic creations of God. It is only in our erroneous thinking that we have set ourselves up as separate, as cut-off from God. God is always there, although, for many people, often in the background. It is the unevolved parts of our psyches (the lower self), and the traffic cop that runs our everyday affairs (the ego mind), that believe we are separate, that believe we are not unique expressions of God. When these aspects of our personality are healed and reoriented to the truth, then the presence of God can become a direct and ongoing experience, and a foreground experience.

Although at first this brief overview of our relationship with God may seem tangential to a discussion about the title of this chapter, which is about "being yourself," it is instead central to finding the courage to being who each one of us really is. For if each of us is an extension of God, if we are an aspect of God made manifest on earth, then it would be disrespectful for us to not be who we really are. If we were someone other than who we really are, then we would deny our true nature as an extension of God.

Each one of us is a divine creation who has at least partially forgotten our true nature. Our spiritual journey involves rediscovering this truth. If we were to genuinely entertain the possibility that we were each a divine creation who has gone astray, who is in the process of coming back to God, then it would be clear that self-responsibility, and being ourselves, are essential keys to rediscovering our true natures. It would also be clear that embracing who we truly are is one of the keys to rediscovering our true connection with God.

If we can accept who we are today—certainly imperfect, in some respects in the dark, often groping and stumbling along, still working on ourselves, etc., and if we can entertain the possibility that our personal problems are a result of our having gone astray, and if we can believe that it is possible for each of us to rediscover our connection with God again, then self-responsibility and the courage to be ourselves will liberate us. When we understand the various aspects of our lower selves, these parts that have separated from God, the parts that have created our problems and discontents, this discovery will strengthen us. Then we can dig into our psyches and look for the self-imposed causes of our pains and discontents. Later, when we connect these causes with the undesirable effects in our lives, we will then be in a position to wipe away all the misconceptions and errors that now stand between us and God.

The lack of inner freedom in our lives is a direct reflection of not wanting to take on self-responsibility, not wanting to be ourselves, and not wanting to do the work necessary to establish our liberation and joy (and liberation and joy both come from a direct connection with God). The more we escape from self-responsibility, from being ourselves, from looking at ourselves, from doing the inner work, the more bound-up and imprisoned we will become.

Having the courage to channel our own unique version of the Divine, or said differently, having the courage to be our divine self, that is in fact in the best interests of others as well. Our joy will be shared with others because we are connected to others. But our stagnation and refusal to grow will hurt not just ourselves -- it will hurt others as well. This only makes sense when we realize that we are connected to others through God.

The more we can each see ourselves as a part of God, as an extension of God, the less trouble will we have in expressing our own unique version of divine consciousness. Each person has their own divine ray, a unique light, a unique gift from the Divine that he or she brings through to the earth. When we can tune into this place, we can use it to help us grow in other areas of our consciousness that are not yet so evolved. When we consciously decide to be a representative of divine consciousness, it is then that it becomes only natural that we should be ourselves. It is then that we can truly perceive the beauty of who we are, and how we are each a creator of our own reality.

Personal Story:

Ariel's stepfather physically abused her sisters when she was growing-up, although she was spared. Partially as a result of this experience, she adopted a strategy to deal with life, which held that she had better constantly defend herself against the next hurtful and unwelcome thing that most likely would soon come along. She went about her life with a chip on her shoulder, saying to others in an energetic way: "I dare you to mess with me." Part of this attitude was also a compensation for her size. As an adult, she stood only 4 feet 10 inches tall.

Quite bright and entertaining, Ariel was nonetheless without a boyfriend for long stretches in her life. When asked about this, and about why she never married, she would simply say, "most of the men out there weren't interesting." But the truth was that most of them were pushed away, deterred from entering into a serious relationship with her because she kept herself so hidden and defended. Behind this behavior, she believed that if she revealed some personal details, then those personal details were most likely going to be used against her. So all of her romantic relationships with men were on a superficial and fleeting basis, which soon bored the men, and as a result, they soon left her.

Still unmarried at the age of fifty, Ariel was on a kayaking vacation in Mexico when she met someone new. This man, who happened to be a psychologist, appreciated her and wanted to know about her inside world. His requests for her feelings, her emotions, her judgments, and her other thoughts confronted her deeply. She appreciated and wanted to believe what this man said about honesty being the path to intimacy and falling in love. She wanted to let go into love, and to create a place of intimate communication, but she dared not go there. After two months of entertaining the possibility of a serious relationship, it became clear to this man that Ariel wasn't going to open up, so he left her.

This was deeply upsetting to Ariel because he was the only man that really captured her imagination, the only serious potential long-term relationship, to come along in over ten years. She had, with her unconscious defenses, pushed him away.

Her fear had triumphed over her heart's desire. But she refused to take this man's "no" for an answer. She frequently called him, sending him gifts and cards, and occasional presents. Although she lived in a distant city, she even showed up at his doorstep repeatedly, each time unannounced, and each time bearing gifts. In response, he consistently said "no" to the prospect of a serious relationship.

The deep hurt from this experience was enough to get Ariel into therapy. Through conversations with her psychiatrist, she was able to see how she had blocked the natural movement, the opening up, of an intimate relationship. After a number of therapy sessions, she came to appreciate how she was hurting herself through her defensiveness, and how she had also hurt this man. Later she came to appreciate how opening up her heart to another person would be a gift to this other person. Although she did not get back together with this man, the brief relationship was instrumental in cracking her heart open, in helping her to let go of the "chip on the shoulder" attitude. At that point she glimpsed what it would be like to have the courage to be her true loving self in an intimate relationship.

Journal Questions:

(1) If you were to genuinely be yourself, whose approval might you need to give up? And what might be the consequences of this giving up? Would it really be so terrible, or perhaps you have made the imagined consequences worse than they would actually be?

(2) If you believe that you must be someone other than your true self, who is this person that you must be? Is he/she a member of some group that you consider to be superior or more desirable? And if the answer is yes, are you not putting yourself up on a pedestal, denying your brotherhood/sisterhood with other humans?

(3) Assume for a moment that you genuinely believe you are an expression of the Divine, a unique light, and possessor of your very own "divine ray." What then would be your artistic and creative expression in the world? How would you paint the canvas of your life? With this perspective, what in your life would you change?

20

Opening to Benefiting from Whatever Happens

Affirmation:

IN THE SPIRIT of giving my best to life and others, of using every moment that life provides for personal growth and personal evolution, I embrace the opportunity that this moment provides. I resolve to use whatever experience I go through as a teaching, as an opportunity to grow.

Core Idea:

Everyone has an unconscious attitude about change, which for most of us remains unexamined. Once they really look at it, and bring it into consciousness, most people appreciate that they have, for a long time, had a fear of movement, or said differently, a fear of change. They have believed that whatever comes next will be worse or less desirable than their present circumstances. They have therefore been holding onto what they have now, with the erroneous belief that by petrifying the current situation, by freezing the current state of their life, they will be able to maintain a relatively pleasant, or relatively known, or at least relatively manageable experience.

This petrified part of the unconscious, which has been lurking in the dark recesses of our consciousness and which has adversely affected our lives, needs to be challenged. It needs to be stirred-up and closely examined in the light of truth. Fortunately, the difficulties and problems of life will naturally stir-up these erroneous views of life, and will present us with an opportunity to examine these issues, as well as an occasion to heal these same issues. In that respect, the difficulties and problems of life are blessings, for without them, these places in us that are not in truth would not be unearthed.

We need to closely scrutinize and question these old and petrified messages about change coming from this part of ourselves. We must determine whether these beliefs are remnants of some past experiences, some painful events or conditions, or perhaps some experiences about which we have over-generalized. If we can adopt an objective and detached viewpoint, examining these beliefs as though they are some strange, and up until recently, unknown part of the unconscious, this will help accelerate our own healing process.

We need to intimately come to know, come to accept, and come to befriend these parts of our unconscious. We need to ask ourselves exactly what they are saying. We need to understand why these parts within us believe it is in our best interest not to change, not to evolve, and not to adapt to new circumstances. Specifically, why is it that these parts keep saying "no" to the changes that we are contemplating? We must use precise language as we formulate the messages from the unconscious— only after we do that can these messages be compared to the now-prevailing truth.

These unconscious messages should also be challenged using a certain point of reference. That point of reference is the truth that when we are giving our best, when we are committed to using every aspect of our life to evolve our consciousness, then, no matter what happens, the events of our lives will, in the long run, will further our personal evolution. In this spirit of total devotion to God, to the truth, to giving all we have to life, we can come to appreciate that no matter what the circumstances of our life may be, those circumstances can always assist us in our personal evolution.

Every earth life problem is actually the expression of a spiritual problem that is begging for our attention. If we solve the problem on the spiritual level, then we can find a true and lasting solution on the earth life level. If we do not solve the problem on the spiritual level, there will be other earth life tests to bring this matter once again to our attention. The specific problem in the world may go away, or become less pressing, but this same type of problem will keep coming back again and again, until the spiritual lesson is learned.

We can ask God to help us understand the spiritual issues behind our problems. We can ask God why we are having such difficulty with a particular issue. We can ask God to help us to understand the spiritual truth, and the way that we may be deviating from that spiritual truth. There is great power in such humble requests for divine assistance. Answers will come, although perhaps not immediately, and perhaps not in the way that we expect or demand.

With such an attitude, every problem we encounter is at least potentially a gift bearing the seeds of the next step in our personal spiritual evolution. With such an attitude, every problem is a message from the spirit world. Thus the successful solving of, or dealing with, every problem increases our happiness and fulfillment. But if we view these problems as unpleasant tasks, as an indication that life is unfairly asking us to do distasteful things we don't want to do, then we miss out on this important opportunity.

Personal Story:

Mercedes grew up in a difficult family situation that was devoid of overt expressions of love and affection. For example, she never witnessed her parents hugging or kissing. Part of that cold environment was a cultural northern European unemotional way of doing things, a way that had been in her family for many generations. This coldness profoundly frustrated Mercedes as a little girl, because she was fundamentally a very loving, emotional, and affectionate person. At some point in her childhood, she gave up trying to get the loving and emotional connection that she wanted from her parents. At this point she also decided that she must go through life as a staunchly independent and self-sufficient person.

Although married twice, and divorced twice, Mercedes had chosen to focus on her career rather than have a family. Part of her had given up on family, and decided that she was never going to get the love, affection, and emotional connection that she yearned for as a child, but never got. No doubt this was part of the reason why she was divorced twice, although she didn't really understand the profound influence that her resolution to be independent had exerted. Nonetheless, there was always something nagging at her, like a missed opportunity, an opportunity to have those things she yearned for, something she turned away from again and again.

When she was in her early fifties, Mercedes got word that her mother was sick with the later stages of ovarian cancer. Her mother's condition worsened quickly, and soon thereafter Mercedes was visiting her mother at her deathbed. The rapidity of the events surrounding her mother's death shocked Mercedes.

Her mother, then in her early seventies, had just retired from a long career, was about to start enjoying her long-saved-for and well-deserved retirement. It upset Mercedes that her mother would never get to enjoy the money she had saved. It upset her that her mother was always putting off her own pleasure, her own desires, her own needs, always metaphorically "saving for a rainy day."

It took the death of her mother to illuminate how Mercedes was like her mother, how she too kept denying the possibility that she could be pleased, satisfied, and supported by her life. Mercedes then came to appreciate that her whole life was influenced by her great desire to prove that she could do everything on her own, that she didn't need anyone. On a deeper level, she saw that she was also getting revenge against her parents, revenge for not giving her the type of love and attention she believed she deserved and needed.

As she was making travel plans to fly to the city where her mother's funeral would take place, Mercedes appreciated how she had been afraid to open her heart to a man. She had been afraid that it would just be another excruciating and painful experience, in much the same way that her childhood was an unbearable and painful experience. This part of her unconscious mind didn't believe that change was possible, this part of her thought she was cursed to always be frustrated in love. When she objectively and dispassionately looked at these beliefs, she was surprised to note at how profound their influence had been on her life. She was also saddened because she saw how she had had multiple opportunities to get the connection, love, and attention that she yearned for, opportunities to which she had repeatedly said "no."

While going through her own grieving process, Mercedes came to appreciate how the death of her mother was a gateway of sorts. The death opened her more deeply to the temporary nature of life, and to appreciating the opportunity that each moment provides. It also helped Mercedes to reach a place where she was much more open to finding and establishing a loving relationship with a man, a relationship that would in fact be a manifestation of her heart's desire.

Journal Questions:

(1) If the change you are having difficulty with were viewed as a gift from the spirit world, how would your attitude shift? How would your approach to the change then be different?

(2) Suppose for a moment that everything we experience ultimately will bring us back to the truth of whom we really are, specifically a divine expression. With this long-term view, there will be no truly bad experiences. If you could for a minute entertain that possibility as it related to the important change that you now seek, could you relax about the process of change?

(3) When it comes to the change that you so ardently seek, could you give up an attachment to having a certain result manifest in your life? Could you stop pushing to have things go in a certain direction? If in fact you were able to do this, how would your energy about the change you seek be considerably different?

21

Holding the Fact That You Will Die

Affirmation:

I ACKNOWLEDGE THAT my days on this earth are numbered, and I resolve to make the most out of my limited time here. I honor each moment, and the opportunity that this moment provides.

Core Idea:

There is a widespread misconception that physical death and pain are the worst things that could possibly happen to a person. Physical death is not a punishment; it is just a fact of life. Physical death is not nearly as bad as many people make it out to be. Much worse is spiritual death, in which a person gives in to the forces of darkness, either consciously or unconsciously. In cases of spiritual death, a person cuts themselves off from God. This is because such a person takes the path of least resistance, gives in to his or her weaknesses, and allows their lower self to run their life.

Far from being a burden, coming to terms with the fact that you will die can spur you on to do what you might not otherwise do. Honestly acknowledging that your days on this earth are numbered underscores the fact that you cannot simply maintain the status quo and hope that your life will turn out. In that state, after every day, you will be that much closer to your death, and every day you are confronted once again with the question: "Why have you not yet done anything about that problem that has plagued you for such a long time?"

Life on earth provides a special opportunity to accelerate our personal development. You can take advantage of that opportunity by overcoming your resistances, by confronting and triumphing over your weaknesses, and by championing your higher self over your lower self. Or you can keep drifting along, in a status quo state not too far different from sleepwalking. Whatever spiritual state you inhabit at the time of your death, this is the state you will be in after you die. Whether in the body or out of it, you will still have to deal with yourself as well as the spiritual state that you are in now.

If you can, at this juncture in your life, adopt a wider vision of your life situation, if you can detach yourself a bit from the day-to-day pressures and tasks, if you can remove yourself from the doing of so many things, then you have a good opportunity to genuinely see what needs to change.

Pray for divine assistance that you may stand in this place of perspective and truth. Be willing to see your life situation clearly, no matter how unflattering it may be. Ask for guidance that you may change yourself and change your life to take advantage of the circumstances that you now face.

Personal Story:

Mitchell was a young man who felt gravely wounded by his nuclear family. He was part of a family in which physical, emotional, and sexual violence had been dominant parts of his early life. As a child, he had no support from his family, and he felt terribly alone. He didn't know what to do with these feelings, but he was certainly aware of the fact that they were very painful, and he no longer wanted to keep feeling them. So, at the age of fourteen, he started to smoke marijuana. He liked the euphoric way he felt after he smoked, and it gave him a respite from his painful feelings of abandonment, loneliness, and isolation.

A relatively smart young man, he was able to keep smoking marijuana, on a regular basis, through high school and college, and at the same time get decent grades. Most days he smoked a joint (a marijuana cigarette) or two. This seemed to do the trick, because his major objective was not to have to feel the pain of his own early family experience. In that respect, he was going with the path of least resistance, he was running from the truth, from the feelings, from the inner reality that he needed to confront, and from an experience that he needed to go through.

After graduation from college, with a major in geology, he felt truly fortunate to get a job with a progressive business that built geothermal energy-generating plants. But within a month of starting his new job, he faced a major decision. The work at the this firm was fast-paced and intellectually demanding, so he had to be on his toes all the time. Mitchell really needed to bring more brainpower to the job than he was then providing. He knew that he must quit smoking marijuana, or else he might soon lose his job. He knew that if he quit the drug, his mental abilities would improve, and he would then stand a better chance of becoming a success in his first permanent full-time job.

Although he didn't like the choice before him, the options were clear, and he chose to quit smoking. His performance at work improved markedly and he really enjoyed this new job. Since he had been smoking pot for so many years, he hadn't realized how many feelings and emotions he had suppressed and sidelined through his smoking habit. Soon thereafter, a lot of difficult issues were coming up for him, and he didn't know what to do with them. He got himself into therapy, and finally started coming to terms with his past. His work situation turned out very well, and he stayed with the firm for five years before being lured away, with a considerably higher salary, by a competing firm.

Journal Questions:

(1) When it comes to that continually vexing problem, in what way have you been acting as though you are never going to die?

(2) If you were going to die in six months, what specific changes would you make in your life? Why not make those changes right now -- regardless of your current health?

(3) Imagine that you have died, and you are looking back on the life you just lived. What opportunities for growth did you miss? What beneficial changes did you refuse to make?

22

Going Beyond Compliance with an Authority

Affirmation:

I AFFIRM MY free will and my freedom to choose the life I want to lead. God wants me to be an independent, aware, and self-responsible adult. God does not want me to be a child who unconsciously complies with the demands of others, as a manipulation, with the hope of getting something in return.

Core Idea:

God demands neither compliance nor obedience. God granted the great gift of free will to human beings so that they can make their own choices about how to live their lives. Of course, if a choice is incompatible with divine law (also known as "the laws of nature"), there will be painful results stemming from this choice. The pain thus created is an indication that something isn't right, that something needs to change. Thus it is through the message behind our pain that we can find our way back to God.

Many religions have, through the ages, demanded both compliance and obedience from their followers. These religions have turned God's dynamic truth into something static and dead, something oppressive and destructive. These religions use dogmas, behavioral creeds, and other rules to control people. The justification for these rules is to protect people against the results that will come from following their own destructive impulses. In this respect, these religions treat people like children, implying that their immature tendencies are uncontrollable, and can only be handled through compliance and obedience to the rigid requirements defined by the religion. Religion does not need to take on the role of law dictation and enforcement, a role that already exists in the civil law area.

One of the most challenging tasks of every human being is overcoming the unconscious part that wishes to remain a child. This part does not want to embrace the hardship implicit in being an adult, does not want to step into true self-responsibility, and does not wish to act in a manner consistent with one's true independence. The child in all of us unconsciously believes it is preferable to remain helpless, and to thereby force others, life, and God to take responsibility for our life. The child in us says: "If I obey and comply, you will protect me, you will make my decisions for me, and then I will be rewarded for being obedient and compliant." Unfortunately, this attitude makes people functionally helpless. To the extent that people don't believe that they have choices, they feel obligated, controlled, disempowered, and then indeed they will be helpless.

A true relationship with God, and life for that matter, involves the personal freedom to choose. This reality-based relationship is the result of self-determined action undertaken in part to understand the truth of one's life. It is the result of our understanding divine law and how it operates in the world. It is important to note that domination, as well as demands for obedience and compliance, are not divine attributes. When you see these in the behavior of others, recognize them for what they are: manipulations and power plays coming from human beings.

Many of us have erroneous ideas about obedience and compliance. We may, for example, have come to believe that if we are obedient and compliant, then we will be "good." This notion may be left over from childhood, or it may come from training in a religious group. Obedience and compliance can be good or bad. For example, following orders handed down by a murderous dictator would be obedient and compliant, but it would not genuinely be good.

What is important is that we appreciate where we are coming from when we act obediently and compliantly. Many of our inner conflicts can be traced to unconscious acts of obedience and compliance that were undertaken in response to an order coming from a human being. When that same order is brought out into the light of day, often it can be seen for what it really is: not worth following.

Regarding following orders, there are many questions we can ask ourselves. We can inquire into the eventual results we are seeking to create through our obedience and compliance. For example, by following orders, we could demonstrate what an exemplary, moral, and upstanding person we are. We may also thereby show how we are superior, or are thereby revealed to be a member of a select group, unlike those who don't act obediently and compliantly. Alternatively, we may be trying to stay out of trouble. Or perhaps we are simply taking the path of least resistance, as would be the case where we may not want to go to the trouble of making up our own mind. Alternatively, we may genuinely be aligned with the intentions of the authority involved, and agree that compliance and obedience is the best course of action.

Rebellion against an authority, particularly habitual rebellion, may also be motivated by unconscious objectives. In this respect, rebellion may be just as restrictive and as unfree as compliance and obedience is. Those of us who are rebelling may simply be in compliance and obedience with another set of principles or rules. One can conform by being obedient and compliant, or by being consistently rebellious and defiant. As is the case for those who are obedient and compliant, to free themselves, rebels need to discover the deeper motivations behind their rebellious and defiant behavior. Then they too may come to see the truth of the situation they face, and they too may then use their free will to choose to change.

Personal Story:

As a middle-aged adult, Richard went through a popular self-actualization course. He greatly benefited from the course, and genuinely thought that other people could also benefit from it too. After the course ended, he was invited to participate in a "leadership program." He aligned himself with this course's stated objective, which was to refine his skills by applying the teachings of the original course. The leadership program also had another objective, which was hidden at the time he enrolled. The concealed objective was to enroll more people in the self-actualization course. In effect, as was later revealed, by participating in the leadership program, Richard became an unpaid salesperson.

The language of the leadership program relied upon a series of very-difficult-to-reach challenges, followed by a series of commitments to live up to those challenges. Although it may have been instructive for a brief period of time to see that one could go beyond his or her self-imposed limits, living up to these challenges was very difficult and time-consuming. After several months, Richard noticed that his performance at work was declining, and that in his relationship with his wife he was feeling increasingly estranged. He was disturbed to realize that he had come to place the many demanding articulated commitments that he had made for the leadership program in the position of top priority in his life.

Participants in the leadership program were urged to "do whatever it takes" in order to meet commitments to enroll a certain number of people in the original course. Those leadership program students who were not willing to play this game were publicly demeaned and guilt-tripped at group meetings. Those not willing to play the game were privately given all sorts of manipulative words, such as being told that they "didn't have what it takes." After a while, Richard came to see that his desire for the approval of other people, and his desire to look good in their eyes, was being grossly manipulated by the teachers in the leadership program.

Richard reached a breaking point with the whole process when he realized that the people teaching the leadership program were operating without integrity. They would constantly promise to do certain things, and then not follow through. He also came to appreciate that the individual needs of the students in the leadership program were not respected, and that students were often treated with distain. For example, some of the teachers saw students as stupid people who would volunteer their time so that others could make money, as people who had been duped into being unpaid salespeople.

Richard then confronted the leadership of the program, telling them that he was no longer willing to participate in an exploitative operation. He also confronted the other participants about their unwillingness to tell the truth about the toll the leadership program had taken in their lives. He furthermore spoke up about how the ulterior motive behind the leadership program had not been disclosed at the time that he enrolled in the program. Richard exercised true leadership at that time because he told the truth and challenged others to do the same.

After resigning from the leadership program, Richard then set about rebuilding his life, the way the airline safety message says that you must first put your mask on before you can help others. Richard realized that he had been neglecting his own self-care because he had been ignoring his feelings about the leadership program. Looking back over the prior six months, he admitted that he had been having misgivings about the program for some time, but he had pushed these feelings aside because he wanted to be accepted and look good. Richard thus found his true leadership by going beyond compliance and obedience with an authority, by coming back to the truth of his personal experience, and the truth of what really mattered to him.

Journal Questions:

(1) In the area where you now have difficulty, if you didn't need to comply with the expectations of anyone, if you

could really follow your heart, if you could follow your deeper calling, what would you do?

(2) Are you experiencing any type of pressure from someone, pressure to choose one particular option in the area where you are having difficulty? Why might this person want you to choose that particular option? Are their reasons to push for a certain option in opposition to your own objectives? If so, specifically in what way are they in opposition?

(3) In what ways are you trying to "be good" (compliant and obedient) when it comes to the area where you now have difficulty? To the extent that you are doing this, is this really compliance with the law of humans, or compliance with the laws of God? If you are being compliant with the laws of humans only, can you now let that go?

23

Claiming Your Right to Self-Government

Affirmation:

I CLAIM THE right to govern my own life, the right to make my own personal choices, and the right to change my circumstances, so that I may unfold and grow in the way which best suits me.

Core Idea:

As children, people are naturally not self-governing. As children, we look to adults for many things, including guidance, knowledge, and protection. As children, we have only a limited consciousness, and that means we are not yet ready to be self-governing. As children, we are unavoidably dependent on adults for the necessities of life, and that too means that children are not yet ready to be self-governing.

Not able to deal with life by himself, a child is afraid of the unknown. Along with the limited consciousness that goes along with life at that age, in an effort to make sense of things, children over-generalize. They make up a rule, they fixate on a particular story, they grab onto something that they believe to be truth. The child seeks the safety that seems to go along with a rock-hard wall of fixedness. This is of course an illusion, because the truth is flexible and always changing.

For example, if following the lead of a parent, and doing things the way the parent dictates produced a sought-after result, such as a loving gesture, then a child may come to believe that he must always please others. Rather than taking self-responsibility, the child then puts the responsibility on the rule that he has developed. Or perhaps, rather than trusting the self to see the truth and make an appropriate situation-specific decision, responsibility is shifted to others, who are then expected to act on the child's behalf and in the child's best interest.

All this is not problematic while an individual is a child, but it becomes problematic when the individual gets older. If an adult (at least in years) has not yet claimed the right to self-government, he will be consumed with resentment. This is because this person's life will be run by fixed rules and/or the dictates of others. For this type of a person, the resentment is toward the self, specifically for not standing up for one's own interests. This adult will lack both self-confidence and self-trust, and may feel unable to make a decision because the rules, or the wishes of others, will be irreconcilably in conflict with the wishes of the self.

If exercised in a selfish way, the practice of self-government can show up as self-will. In a state of limited self-awareness, an individual can operate with a duality which claims that either the individual governs his or her own life, or the individual relinquishes control and entrusts himself to God. But in a state of greater awareness, a place of we-are-all-one-in-God, a person can come to appreciate that self-government and self-accountability are in fact necessities for a deeper connection to God. This is because such an aware adult consciously chooses to align with God, and also consciously chooses to take responsibility for the ways in which he is out of alignment with God. Thus when an adult has this wider awareness, he desires to expand and refine his own self-responsibility, and that causes him to undertake efforts to adjust so as to better align himself with God.

Thus, using one's will in the service of selfishness (thinking only of the self, doing only as one pleases, manipulating others to get one's way, etc.) is a hindrance to both mature self-responsibility and self-governance. But using one's will in the service of a broader objective, in the service of God and the truth fosters self-responsibility, which in turn fosters self-governance. Only when we step up to true self-responsibility and true self-governance can we powerfully act as agents of the truth, as agents for God on earth.

Said differently, to the extent that an individual embraces his connection with all that is, including a connection with God, to the extent that he is unified in intention and in self-concept, to that extent no conflict will exist between one's own will and the will of the Divine. This inner alignment can only take place when an individual sees, meets, and accepts all their inner aspects. Then an individual can make conscious choices about how to think and act, and these choices will in turn change how the individual feels and reacts.

Thus there is an aware state, where the individual has the right, the ability, in fact the requirement, to both exercise and claim self-government to make personal choices. In this state of inner awareness, the choices one makes are compatible with the choices that God would want, because there is no perceived separation between the self and God. Thus making personal choices, and asserting one's right to self-government, when coming from this place, will bring divine consciousness further into the world.

Personal Story:

Laurie grew up in a religious household where great emphasis was placed on self-sacrifice. Her family taught her that sacrificing one's own desires, so as to serve another, was a desirable and loving way to act. When she was in college, she met a man named Maurice for whom she developed a crush. Maurice was busy with his own life, and didn't pay much attention to Laurie. She tried flirting with him, but that didn't produce the desired result, specifically an invitation to go on a date or some other indication of his romantic interest.

Laurie decided that she needed something a bit more dramatic. Maurice was studying computer science, so she reasoned something to do with computers might be of interest to him. Laurie's best friend, Jane, worked in the registrar's office, and as part of her job, Jane had access to the computerized records of all students at the college. Laurie pressured Jane to make a copy of Maurice's record, so that she might know his birthday, and thereby become able to send Maurice a birthday card. Jane resisted, citing the college's privacy policy as a good reason not to comply with the request. Laurie went into an involved explanation about what it means to be unselfish, and also how this would "really mean a lot" to her. By making a big deal about being her best friend, and talking about "what friends do for each other," Laurie guilt-tripped Jane into giving her Maurice's computerized record.

It turned out that Maurice's birthday was only a few weeks from the date when Jane turned over the record to Laurie. Laurie was able to send a birthday card to Maurice, and it did indeed get his attention. Maurice was a bit disturbed that Laurie knew his birthday, a type of information that he thought was private, and he asked her how it was that she obtained to this information. Laurie did not respond in a specific way, hoping that a coy answer would intrigue Maurice. While Maurice was impressed that Laurie was resourceful and clearly interested in him, the relationship didn't go anywhere romantically.

Instead, Maurice went on to complain to the college administration, and they launched an investigation into the circumstances leading up to the disclosure of his private academic records. When the facts came to light, Jane admitted violating the privacy policy, and as a result, she lost her part-time job with the registrar's office.

Like Laurie, Jane had believed that love meant submission to another. In fact, this situation was not evidence of Jane's love for Laurie; it was instead evidence of Jane's emotional bondage. Jane did not assert her right to self-determination and self-government, and as a result, she suffered not only a financial setback, but also a severe blow to her relationship with Laurie. The incident was actually quite helpful to Jane, because it helped her to see that submission, and catering to the demands and whims of another, is not love. She came to appreciate that love includes self-government, and that love does not require that she follow the instructions of another. Laurie also benefited from this experience in that she was, after that incident, more respectful of the ways in which her requests might be disadvantageous to others, as well as more respectful of the right of others to say "no" to her requests.

Journal Questions:

(1) If you were to let go of the notion that you are a helpless victim, if you were to make your own decisions based on your own inner truth, that is if you were to exercise true self-government, what new choices would you make? Make a list of at least five new choices you would make.

(2) Mature self-government requires that an individual give up greedy, childish, selfish, and arrogant ways. Mature self-government makes choices which are in keeping with the all-encompassing-truth, choices which are in the best long-run interests of all involved. How could your self-will push you to act in greedy, childish, selfish, and arrogant ways? What specifically does it do to manipulate you?

(3) If you are now aware of how the child inside you would push you to act (from your answer to the question immediately above), and if you can then be vigilant about and compensate for this, why is it that you still refrain from taking on the mantle of mature self-government? What specifically is the fear or negative intention that blocks you from taking this step?

24

Deciding Truly for Yourself

Affirmation:

As an INDEPENDENT adult, I am the one to decide how I will show up in life. I am no longer required to fall into step with the dictates of my parents and other caregivers, as was the case when I was a child. As an adult, I embrace my right to go my own way.

Core Idea:

Many people hold opinions and beliefs that are not their own. They simply adopt these ways of dealing with life without really thinking about them. Often this approach is dictated by the fear of appearing to be different. The prospect of being unique, of being notably different than others, seems both scary and dangerous. To be different is then imagined to be a source of great shame. And so these people go to great lengths in order to conform.

If a child adopts such a conforming approach to life, it is understandable, because a child is dependent on adults (primarily the parents, but also other family members, teachers, babysitters, and others), and is therefore in need of the approval of these same adults. In most instances, a young child has not yet developed a strong ego, with which she could withstand and deal with the negative judgments of others. For the young child, compliance often seems to be the best survival strategy. The trouble comes when people are adults, but they are still using this childhood strategy for dealing with life.

Complying with the desires and expectations of others is a pseudo-solution for dealing with life (the word "pseudo" is appropriate because the strategy doesn't really work). For an adult who still holds onto this childhood strategy, there is often an exaggeration of the difference between themselves and others, and an exaggeration of the importance of this difference. This exaggeration is blown way out of proportion if adults don't talk about this matter with others, and thus receive much-needed reality testing. Keeping all this inside is often the way things go because these adults are ashamed of this part of themselves. But there is nothing to be ashamed of here; it's just another part of us that needs to grow up.

This blowing out of proportion of one's differences from others is often accompanied by an inability to constructively receive and seriously consider criticism. When we engage in this type of self-talk, we affirm our fragility, and we hypnotize ourselves into the belief that we are not able to deal with the feedback that life would bring. So out of our belief in our weakness, we opt to conform, to do what public opinion says we should, and to not disappoint others. But in the process we sell ourselves out, and we betray our own truth. In this process, we deny reality, which is that in some ways we are like others, and in some ways we are different.

The solution is not to be rebellious and do the opposite of what others suggest. That would be just as tied to their opinions as conformity is. Likewise, the solution is not to be unconcerned with the opinions of others. We must of course get along with and work with others, so their opinions are important. But to make conformity to the opinions of others a type of bondage is equivalent to keeping ourselves on a short leash; it is treating ourselves as though we were some sort of unruly and untrainable dogs. To treat ourselves in this way is neither kind nor loving, nor is it embracing the truth of who we could be—it simply tries to make the best of what we understand to be our situation, using the strategy that we knew as a child.

The solution is to deeply examine our own opinions, to know our own personal truth, to go our own way, knowing full well there will be consequences, but at the same time being willing to deal with those consequences. A free person is willing to go without positive public opinion, or even the positive opinions of loved ones, in order to be true to herself. A healthy and free adult takes the time to discover her own truth, and then clearly knows what she wants. Such a person knows that there will be a price to be paid for following these desires, and she is willing to pay that price.

Personal Story:
Zeke was raised in a very strict household, a family environment where his "career military man" father had formal written rules and standards. There was very little room for personal expression in Zeke's family, if that expression fell outside the rules and standards dictated by his father. Although he did get a good high school education, and he felt safe in his home, Zeke also felt profoundly stifled and hemmed-in. He felt as though he had to always walk the straight and narrow path, and that he must never deviate from the accepted way of doing things. In high school, Zeke had a profound fear of making his own way through life. He would typically hang back, wait to see what other people did, and then follow suit. As a result of this fearful behavior, Zeke was taunted and teased by some other boys, who would often call him "sissy boy."

When he first went away to college, Zeke was disoriented and lost. In this new and free environment, he didn't have his father breathing down his neck, telling him what to do. As a result, he went wild. He got involved with a lot of binge drinking, took many different types of illegal mind-altering drugs, had casual sex with a bunch of women, and in general didn't take care of himself. In college, there was a part of Zeke that was in rebellion. His statement to the world could be summed up by the words: "You're not going to tell me what to do." Although he acted out with great pleasure, doing things that he knew his father would not approve of, he also felt guilty because he sensed that he was, as he put it, "screwing-up his life in a big way."

When the first semester freshman year's grades came in, he knew he was in serious trouble. Zeke got one B, two Cs, and a D. He knew that not only would his father be furious, but that he would lose his scholarship if he didn't maintain at least a B+ average. Then, while he was at home over the holidays between semesters, Zeke developed pains in his jaw. After seeing a dentist, it came to light that Zeke had not been regularly brushing his teeth, and that he had several very serious cavities on his lower left side. The bad grades, the words of warning from his father, and the serious dental problems all convinced him that he had better make some major changes to the direction in which he was going.

Working with his journal, he endeavored to get a handle on what was happening. Through some introspection, Zeke was able to determine that he had shifted his compliance with his father's opinions to compliance with the opinions of his new set of wild partying friends. But no matter who Zeke was listening to, he had still been simply following along. He really didn't know what he wanted, and he hadn't taken the time to discover what his personal truth was. Based on his investigations, Zeke decided that he needed time to discover his own truth, and that he didn't want to prematurely end his college experience.

So Zeke set out to discover what he wanted, as best he understood it right then. He didn't know what he wanted to study, what kind of a job he wanted later in life, or even whether he wanted to have a wife and children. All he really knew was that he didn't want his options to be prematurely terminated. Zeke knew that he wanted to lovingly give himself the time and space to discover what he was good at, what he wanted to do, and what kind of a life he wanted to manifest. There was no question that the best way to keep his options open, the way to give himself some space to discover these things, was to stay in school, stay on his scholarship, and be diligent when it came to his studies.

The next semester was a very different experience for Zeke. Not only did he find other friends who were looking toward their futures instead of the next wild party, but he also started taking care of himself. He got his teeth fixed, made an effort to get enough sleep, and started working out by lifting weights. He spent a lot of time studying and learning about what his future might look like. This felt like more of an adult experience to Zeke, where he was being a leader in his own life, instead of just falling in line and following other people. As a result of taking the time to investigate what he really wanted, Zeke felt much more grounded in his life, and as might be expected, his grades markedly improved as well.

Journal Questions:

(1) Is there any part of your desire to stay where you are— to not make the change that you consciously say you want—which is motivated by the need to conform to an established way of doing things? If so, what is this place

inside you saying? Exactly why does that place inside you believe that you need to conform?

(2) Who in your life might have a problem with the change that you are contemplating? Exactly why would that be problematic for each of these people? Have you spoken about the possibility of this change with these people? Have you engaged in a conversation for a new possibility with them? If not, why not?

(3) Imagine for a moment that you went your own way, that you bucked the opinions of others, and that you went ahead and made the change that you deeply yearn for. What would the fallout be (the negative reactions and negative repercussions)? Realistically speaking, could you handle this fallout?

25

Standing Up to Discouragement and Self-Doubt

Affirmation:

ANYTHING IS POSSIBLE with God. I ask for divine assistance so as to see clearly how I contribute to my experience of discouragement, self-doubt, and other negative feelings. I ask for the vigilance and perseverance that I may catch myself when I fall into these feelings, so that instead I may choose to align with God, truth, and personal evolution.

Core Idea:

The days when we feel discouraged and doubtful are very important ones. During these times we make a series of choices to fall prey to our faults, those parts of our lower self that dominate and control us. Instead, we could choose to grow, evolve, change, come into truth, and align ourselves with God. It is important that we acknowledge what choices we make, because often our destructive habits have become so ingrained that we don't consciously think about these choices. In these critical times, we should notice how we have given in to these moods, and how easily we allow these faults to control us and keep us stuck where we are. To not give in to these faults is a habit that must be cultivated if we are going to successfully shift our viewpoint, if we are going to build confidence, and if we are going to develop a grounded faith that we can indeed make a desired change.

In these moments when we are being tested—and by the way when we fall into these foul moods we are indeed being spiritually tested—then it is imperative that we illuminate exactly what these faults are that are controlling us. We must know what we are fighting against if we are going to be successful with the grand fight. So often we acknowledge that we are having trouble, but we don't take the next step to clarify what exactly it is that we are fighting. So often these moods descend upon us, uninvited, unwanted, and seemingly out of nowhere. To the extent that we adopt this "I'm not causing this" attitude, to that same extent do we allow these faults to continue to dominate us, to run our lives, to keep us stuck in a painful place.

What we are talking about here is forming a new habit, a constructive and positive habit, one that keeps the door open to a new way to be in life, a habit that empowers us to engineer the changes that we desire. In these moments, we must ask God for help, ask that we might clearly know why we are feeling so low and discouraged. In these moments, we must ask for God's truth, the objective truth, the all-encompassing truth, the broader understanding that contextualizes both what we are doing and how we are being. We need to ask God for an understanding of His will for us, and we must be open to receiving His answer, whatever that answer might be. This request and the open willingness to receive any answer, accompanied by a neutrality with respect to the answer, must collectively be undertaken with utter sincerity. If we do not sincerely seek that result, we must first look at what in us stands in the way of asking with utter sincerity.

Everything that we suffer from, everything that causes us pain and discomfort comes to us directly or indirectly from our faults, from our lower self, from the parts in us that need to evolve. This is the origin of all of our fears. It is within our power to break the chains that hold us bound-up with our lower self, the chains that hold us in a pattern in which we are at the mercy of our own faults. But we must believe that we can break out of these chains, and that we can confront and change those parts of our lower self that are causing us trouble. If we do not believe in this possibility, we must first address why we are not yet open to even believing in this possibility. Only when that important hurdle is successfully cleared, can we fruitfully employ this new habit in our personal development process.

We each have the strength to confront these aspects of our lower selves. No matter what our personal circumstances may be, every human being has that strength. But to use this great power, we must believe that we possess it. God has not given any of us a task that we cannot perform. If we doubt this, in our prayers we need to ask God if this is true. If we believe that the change we are called to make is too much for us, we must truly confront why we would hold this viewpoint. Believing that the big change we desire is too much for us is a mind game, an ego trick, just another way that our lower self keeps us stuck.

The lower self wishes to remain in the shadows. The lower self is lazy, and it does not like to change. Whenever we look at our lower selves with a metaphorical magnifying glass, we make it uncomfortable, and one of the first responses it predictably will have is the assertion, "I can't do this." We need to confront that claim, and honestly examine whether there is any justification for such a claim.

It is in the commitment to establish and maintain this good habit, where we confront our lower selves, where we stop our lower selves from repeatedly dragging us down into bad moods, into places of discouragement and doubt—that is the place where we all need discipline. Maintaining this commitment with tenacity is important in order to show ourselves that there really is a whole new way of operating and it does in fact work for us. To continue to maintain this commitment, to keep mustering our positive intention to give our best to this effort—that is the type of spiritual discipline we need in order to create this very important new habit.

It is true that our ego cannot accomplish this big change alone, when it is operating in isolation, as long as it holds itself in a place separated from God. Therefore, to be successful with the process of changing, we must ask for and be willing to receive divine assistance. We must ask for help to tenaciously stick with the process, to see it all the way through, to be willing to do the dirty work. We must also be willing to confront all of the many aspects of the truth about our situation, and to be willing to stand up to our lower selves. We must be willing to do these things again and again, as long as necessary, in order to bring about the big change that we desire.

All things are possible with God, as long as these things are compatible with divine law, are good for all concerned, can bring you back to God, and are compatible with God's will for you and your life. For you to discover a new place of faith and connection with God, so that you can then overcome and transform your lower self, that is absolutely compatible with divine law. For you to evolve yourself and come closer to God is also good for everyone involved. For you to build your personal faith in God and the process of life, because you have discovered the truth in you, and because you have successfully overcome and transformed your lower self, that too is compatible with God's will for you and your life. For you to go ahead and make the changes that God is asking of you, absolutely that too is in keeping with God's will for you and your life.

Personal Story:

Victor was a young immigrant man who was still trying to get accustomed to the American way of doing things. As he understood it, having a fancy car, expensive clothes, a big apartment in a good neighborhood, and a high-paying job were all the marks of a successful life in America. In response to the messages that he got from TV, movies, books, and friends, he bought a used but still very expensive German luxury car. He also rented a pricey condominium, bought a wardrobe of fancy clothes, and got his hair cut by a high-end local stylist. He didn't have the money for all of this, so he went into significant credit card debit. In order to make the payments on the debt, he was working three jobs. He was a pizza deliveryman, a health club front desk clerk, and a part-time house remodeling construction hand.

After a while, all the many hours of work and all the bills seemed like a pointless exercise. Yes, he was able to seduce a few American women because they initially thought he was rich. It was a hollow experience, however, because he was, after all, deceiving them, and they soon discovered his true financial situation. After he read more about the business structure of American society, he came to appreciate that most businesses wanted him to buy things, so they attempted to convince him that buying products and services was somehow going to make him happy.

Through his own introspection, he inquired into the true cause of his unhappiness. After reading some books about happiness and spiritual growth, he came to see that he had been seduced into believing that if he selfishly enjoyed the "good things of life," then he was going to be happy. He started to play with the notion that his true happiness would instead come through his personal growth, and also through making a contribution to others.

The charge of energy and the elation that came about as he discovered these things astounded Victor, and he knew he wanted more of these epiphanies. He made a decision to explore why he felt that his life was pointless and meaningless. Continuing to examine why his thoughts caused him to feel certain ways brought forth many new revelations. For example, he came to appreciate that he was creating meaning for himself through the process described here. He also came to appreciate that he created meaning for himself when he shared his personal development process, and the insights thus gained, with others. He came to appreciate how he was ultimately responsible for his own personal experience on earth, and this spurred him on to discover the causes of his experience.

Soon thereafter, he sold his fancy German car, moved to a much less expensive apartment with roommates, and started to live within his means. It took Victor a few years to pay off all the debt he had incurred. He knew he was a good worker, and at times in the past, as circumstances required, he had worked hard (in the bean fields, for example). He was surprised that he could seriously and tenaciously work to embrace the truth of his situation, and work with dedication to return to a balanced lifestyle that was within his means. During that time in his life, he felt surprise that he had no interest in working hard to impress women.

A short while after he started changing his lifestyle, Victor met a woman who didn't care about all the fancy trappings of a rich guy, but instead was interested in who he was, including his insights about life. Last we heard, he has been in a loving, honest, and intimate relationship with her for six years.

Journal Questions:

(1) In order to pull off the masks and pretenses that allow your lower self to continue to run your life, let your most recent complete day pass in front of your mind's eye, as if it were a movie in very fast motion. Ask yourself where you had a disharmonious or discouraged feeling, or perhaps a moment of self-doubt. Choose one such moment, preferably the most emotionally potent of these. No matter what the other person(s) did in this situation, ask God where you might have contributed to the negative feelings or the negative result. Do this daily over the course of several weeks, perhaps in the evening before you go to sleep, going deeper with the process over time, until patterns come forward.

(2) For a week, take ten to fifteen minutes each day to go within, to have a conversation with God. Use this time to ask about how you might have unconsciously contributed to the negative feelings and negative situations that you experience. If you cannot do this, what is standing in the way? What is the story that you tell yourself, and is that same story, on a deeper level, actually true?

(3) If you keep falling into a mood of discouragement, self-doubt, and similar negative feelings, but you keep pushing those feelings aside, without examining them, without probing your own depths to identify their causes, why is that? Why do you keep making a choice to allow your lower self to run its number, to play its game of evasion, over and over?

26

Stepping Out of the Hopeless or Perfect Paradigm

Affirmation:

IF I HAVE not yet manifested my goal, life is telling me that there is still more work to be done. I am willing, able, and committed to do the required work, whatever that may be.

Core Idea:

As is the case with many aspects of life, most humans live in a duality when it comes to getting what they want. On the one hand, they feel as though it is hopeless, and that they might as well give up all further attempts to manifest what they desire. On the other, they feel elated because, at least for a brief while, life seems to give them what they want. Over the course of their life, they can repeatedly move back and forth from one end of this duality to the other.

Although we intellectually would all agree that of course life does not always give us what we want, on an emotional level we do not want to accept this fact. We each need to closely examine what it is that we feel when frustrated by life. Do we, for example, fall into a place where we beat ourselves up, saying words like, "I am so bad," or "I cannot overcome these weaknesses that I have"? With such a frame of mind, many of us fall into a place of sloth and giving up, a place where we in fact increase the likelihood of being frustrated, because we do not devote our positive energies to the manifestation of the circumstances we desire.

This place of hopelessness, when examined more closely, often reveals our pride and arrogance. Many of us childishly believe that we should have our sought-after circumstances handed to us—as if we were still a child, and as if some other person was going to do the necessary work for us. With this attitude, many of us wish to be more evolved, more capable, and more competent, than we are now. We want to be perfect, yet we don't want to mount the effort to move in the direction of perfection. We don't want to admit that we are not yet perfect, because this would wound our pride, and this would damage our vanity.

One way to avoid having to confront these unflattering places within us is to deny what is really going on. In this place we maintain a charade that everything is perfect in our life. We give the impression that what we have right now is what we wanted. In this place, we act as though we are happy, when deep down we know it is not true. This is a dangerous practice because it can lead to repression of our feelings, and these feelings can then sink into the unconscious (that is until they are provoked to come forward again by life's challenges). Avoidance and denial of the truth is a serious mistake, because it engenders more problems and conflicts, which then make life still more painful and difficult.

We can consider another way to be, a way outside this duality of hopelessness or perfection. In this place, we can accept our current circumstances, including our current state of consciousness, as our temporary reality. We can become clear about what it is that we want to create, and how it differs from the current reality. In this place, we know that creating the circumstances we desire requires struggle, willpower, focus, and patience. We can realize that creating the life we want will require us to take many small and constructive steps in that direction. In this place we realize that adopting an attitude of hopelessness will only block us from undertaking these constructive next steps.

Personal Story:

Harold came from a well-known family that had, in prior generations, been successful in business, and made a great deal of money. As a result, he enjoyed a privileged childhood, growing up on a large farm with two brothers and a sister. The adults in his family were often talking about a particularly famous family member, all the while insinuating that Harold would of course grow up to be like that man. For Harold, the pressure to grow up to be larger than life, to become some great leader, was intense.

While he was in high school, Harold was often teased, tormented, and beat up by bullies. Physically on the heavy side, Harold avoided sports and tended to be a bookworm. His repeated problems with bullies were in some ways similar to his relationship with his father. Harold would often feel censored, repressed, and dictated to by his father, so he would rebel by acting like a clown, and indirectly mock his father. This did not go down well with his father, who consequently often punished Harold, while the other two sons and the daughter suffered no such punishment. Similarly, Harold would sass the bullies at school, and his disrespectful attitude got him into even worse trouble with the bullies. The perverse part about this behavior pattern was that Harold did this same thing again and again. Harold erroneously believed that if he successfully annoyed those who he believed to be his adversaries, then he was winning the game of life.

Although he was relatively intelligent, and he could have made more of a contribution to others over the years, Harold retreated into a fantasy world of his own making supported by books. Because he had a trust fund paying a modest annuity every year, he was able to, and actually did stop working at a young age. The majority of his adult life was spent largely hiding in his fantasy world, which nobody really knew much about. When he did present himself in public, Harold was often verbally abusive, in a mocking kind of way, or at the very least was grotesquely inappropriate with his words. These behaviors not surprisingly meant that he had no friends, except for two loyal men who had known him since high school, men who contacted him a few times a year just to check up on him.

In Harold's mind he could not possibly live up to the grandiose expectations of his family, so he wasn't even going to try. This sense of hopeless futility was cemented into place by his rebelliousness and vindictiveness. His cruel and punishing words distanced him from people, and this only underscored and perpetuated the hopelessness of his situation. Harold continued in this no-man's-land of life for decades, waiting for a hoped-for better life, a life that he imagined would arrive when he inherited a significant amount of money from his father.

Soon after Harold's father finally died, at a ripe old age of ninety-three, Harold was very disappointed to learn that he had inherited virtually nothing. The very large farm and the bulk of his father's assets went to his sister. In some respects, his father's death was a wake-up call, underscoring the fact that Harold had done little with his life, and that he had been essentially a miserable hermit for decades.

At this point in his life, Harold was in his late sixties, and living in an assisted living facility. Soon after this realization, he started to read stories to other people living in the same facility, especially those who had lost their sight. Through this reading he found a new satisfaction in the simple companionship that this type of service provided. He was amused that he had employed his many years of reading, and his extensive knowledge of literature, to create a new way to contribute to others. Surprisingly, the readings brought a new joy to his life. This new role seemed much more real and satisfying than the mental battle he had been waging within, a battle in which he had been endlessly moving back and forth between being a "good boy" and a heroic rebel.

Journal Questions:

(1) When it comes to the sought-after goal that you are having trouble achieving, to what extent have you decided that to give up is humble, modest, or realistic?

(2) In this same area, what prevents you from using all possible avenues to approach that same goal? What is the story you are telling yourself, a story that advises you against giving this goal everything you've got?

(3) If you were to manifest this sought-after goal, would you be required to act or behave with a high standard? And does this high standard discourage you from even attempting to manifest the goal? If so, is it really true that this high standard must be met? And if indeed this is so, is it really going to be as difficult as you imagine?

27

Avoiding the Depression and Disappointment of Backsliding

Affirmation:

I RESOLVE TO do what it takes to accomplish this change, and also to be vigilant, lest I fall back into my old ways, unconsciously, out of habit, or simply because I am not paying attention. What's different now is that I have the perspective and intention that together allow me to keep choosing a new way. If I do backslide, I will keep picking myself back up, keep dusting myself off, keep working at it, until this new way becomes my new habit, and becomes my accustomed way to be in the world.

Core Idea:

To let go of a long-held idea about the world, to let go of a long-practiced habit, to let go of a long-experienced way to live—that kind of change does not happen suddenly. It is not as though a person can make up her mind to change, and then all of a sudden everything is consistently different from that point forward. There will be a transition period, a time when we are repeatedly tested. As much as we might not like it, there is no shortcut. Making an important change takes diligent work, and it takes commitment. When it's relevant, it also takes the humility to admit that one has fallen back into the old ways.

To backslide, to revert to the old and less desirable way of doing things happens to many of us. The human psyche is habit-bound, and it is accustomed to functioning in a certain way. It takes a while to reliably establish a new way of being. We shouldn't be ashamed if we're having trouble with this transition. Such trouble is a natural and ordinary part of the process. Each instance of backsliding is a test of our resolve, a test to determine whether we are serious about making the big change that we seek.

The hard part is to remain vigilant, to stay on guard, so that we notice in subtle and at first minor ways, how we are falling back into the old and less desirable way of operating. We must constantly watch ourselves, and observe how we function when operating in the new way. In hidden and perhaps not outwardly noticeable ways, we may be reverting back to our old ways. We must accept that this reversion to old ways is a very real possibility for us, and that to prevent this reversion, we must constantly be on the lookout. We must also be committed to nipping these problems in the bud before they go on to become serious issues.

We can, for example, be going through the physical motions associated with a new way to be, but internally we can be dragging our feet. We need to monitor our inner state regarding the transition process, specifically noticing where we have an upset, a disharmony, or a block. We must work with these impediments to the change process, bring them to conscious awareness, and squarely confront the truth about what we think and feel. Only with this inquiring, attentive, and diligent approach can we ferret out and deal with the remaining impediments to successfully making the big change that we seek.

If we do not realistically approach the change process in this manner, knowing that there will be remnants of the old way of operating, then we are unwittingly setting ourselves up for depression and disappointment. If we think that as soon as we see the big picture, as soon as we genuinely resolve to change, then the whole world will show up differently from that point forward, we are bound to be both depressed and disappointed. This is a fantasy with only two options: either we are instantly complete with our change process, or else the whole process of change is a farce and totally useless. The truth is somewhere in between. After embracing this in-between grey area, we can then find the tenacity to keep going, and in the process gradually build a realistic belief that the change we seek is in fact possible.

To most successfully apply this approach as a spiritual discipline, we can, before we go to bed, briefly meditate about where we may have been backsliding during the prior day. To speed the change process, we should ask ourselves some questions like: "Where did I have a problem, an issue, an upset, a disharmony, associated with the new way of operating?" Then, to accelerate our process, we should briefly write about our experiences, and how it was that these experiences came to manifest. When doing this, we should ask for divine guidance, and ask to see where we helped to cause these experiences, in what way we were responsible for these experiences, and how we could change for the better. In this same daily review process, we should also uncover our deeper intentions and ask for help to purify them, so that the next time we encounter similar circumstances we can come from a more evolved place. We should furthermore ask to know how we may have been out of truth, where we may have violated spiritual law, and what part within us still needs to change and evolve.

Personal Story:

Melissa was forty-years-old, and she very much wanted to get married and have children. She often spoke about a family scenario, and dreamed about it a great deal. At the time of this snapshot, she was divorced from her first husband, and there was no man currently in her life who seemed like a good future husband. During the last five years, Melissa had gone through a series of relationships with a variety of men, who she claimed, had all misled her about the nature of their involvement with her. As she explained her situation to others, these men were all initially playing up to her dream, but later it was revealed that none of them had a serious interest in becoming involved with her in a long-term relationship.

When she really confronted the reality of what was re-peatedly happening, Melissa was depressed and crestfallen. Each of the men she had dated since her divorce had seemed so exciting, so much as though they were ideal, so much as though they were "the one" to help her manifest her dream of a having family. In a series of sessions with her personal coach, Melissa clearly saw how she had viewed each of these men as Prince Charming, who was offering her the perfectly-fitting slipper, straight out of the classic Grimm Brothers' fairy tale called Cinderella. As she saw it, Melissa had done whatever was needed to fit her foot into the slipper, so as to magically create the fantasy life she yearned for.

For example, she would instantly change her work schedule, and so inconvenience her clients, to be able to go on romantic out-of-town trips with these men, if the men asked her to do so. She would go for days without talking to these men, if they expected her to do that, although these long stretches without communication caused her great inner turmoil. Melissa would also lend the men money, if they asked that of her. She would do anything it took to prove that this particular man of the moment was "the one," and that she was the Cinderella whose foot perfectly fit the slipper. With this attitude of doing anything to get her foot to fit into the slipper, and of forcing the man to be "Mr. Right," Melissa was actually more like one of the nasty stepsisters in the Cinderella story, rather than she was like Cinderella herself.

Melissa's process was predictable and her friends could tell you the stages she would go through: (1) after meeting a new man, she would fall in love and become convinced that this guy was "the one"; (2) she would soon thereafter act as though she and this man were together as a committed couple; (3) she would deny and ignore many pieces of evidence that contradicted her wishes and assumptions; and (4) she would finally accuse each of these men of lying to her and deceiving her, and then immediately thereafter she would break off the relationship.

With her life coach, Melissa admitted that she might actually have some responsibility, instead of always blaming the men for lying to her, for misleading her, for not living up to her high standards for them. She saw that, in her eyes, these men were either Prince Charming or they were lying, cheating, and deceiving imposters. She saw how she had been playing a relationship game where it was either "my way or the highway." This game demanded that men show up exactly the way she wanted them to, and she ignored all the evidence indicating that the men did not show up in exactly that way, until the evidence became overwhelmingly obvious and undeniable. This game was dictated entirely by Melissa, a game to which no man had explicitly agreed, a game without mutuality, and a game without any give and take between the participants.

After Melissa saw the big picture, saw how she had been playing this game repeatedly, she admitted to her coach that she understood she would never manifest a family as long as she continued with the game. Soon after that realization, she met a smart and handsome man who was interested in her, and in having a family. She took the relationship slowly, got to know him, realized he wasn't yet ready to commit, and realized that he too was getting to know her. Although she was still in process with this man when we lost touch with her, she was delighted that she could step into and inhabit the grey area, delighted that she could go through the intermediate steps of gradually building intimacy, instead of demanding that all the work be already done, and that she magically and immediately be given what she wanted without having to do any work. Two years later, her coach received an invitation to her wedding, and although the coach did not attend, sure enough, Melissa did manifest her dream of getting married to this same man.

Journal Questions:

(1) What same old habit pattern do you exhibit when you backslide, when you go back to the old and less desirable way of being? Why is it that you keep falling into a repetition of that habit? What is your deeper intention when you do fall back into it?

(2) When you backslide with respect to the change you seek to make, or if you have not yet done that, when you backslide with respect to other changes you seek to make in your life, what emotional reaction do you have? Are you impatient? Do you beat yourself up? Do you feel discouraged?

(3) Are you genuinely inwardly resolved to completely go through a period of uninterrupted effort, a period of vigilant perseverance, a phase in which you keep working to overcome what you must overcome in order to manifest the big change that you seek? If you are not genuinely resolved to do this, resolved to do all that it takes in order to change, why not?

28

Finding an Alignment
of Different Aspects of
Your Consciousness

Affirmation:

MY LIFE EXPERIENCE precisely reveals those places where I
am in a state of inner conflict. I now choose to look more
closely at this feedback from life. I am identifying those places
that are in conflict, unifying those parts within me, and also
unifying with God.

Core Idea:

The human struggle to find meaning and fulfillment is in
large measure so difficult because every person is disconnected from parts of his own consciousness. People are not aware

of all these different parts (which include some lower-self aspects and also some higher-self aspects), and this not knowing needlessly engenders fear. In the last analysis, all fears are derived from this central fear, the fear of fully meeting oneself. As long as people keep part of themselves unknown or hidden, they cannot possibly be free, and they cannot possibly step into their full potential.

The process of purifying one's consciousness—which roughly involves bringing every part into the light, truing it up with reality, aligning it with the higher self, and aligning it with God— that process cannot proceed unless a person is willing to tackle and deal with every last bit of straying consciousness. This process involves exposing everything within, at least to God, and hiding no part of one's consciousness. In the process of this purification, choices will be made to evolve, to mature, to become more competent in life, and these choices help to precipitate the alignment and the unification, of these inner parts.

This process of alignment and unification of all parts of our consciousness is the natural and organic direction in which life leads us. But we block the process with our unnecessary fear of self. Having a fear of self inevitably leads to a state of self-alienation, a state of being disconnected from various parts of oneself. Another byproduct of this process is stagnation—a sense of being mired in the mud of life. This fear of self is unnecessary because all it is, at its most fundamental level, is a fear that we will not be all we thought we should be. Such a fear is unrealistic because we are all obviously imperfect beings, and we are all in the process of evolving ourselves.

If we increase the degree of alignment among different aspects of our consciousness, our power to manifest will markedly expand. This approach holds the key to personal evolution because through the discovery of additional aspects of your consciousness (hidden intentions buried in the unconscious, for example), you come more fully into a position of self-responsibility for your life experience. The more levels of consciousness about which you are aware, the faster can you change your consciousness. The faster you can shift your consciousness, the faster your life can change. And the faster you can change your life, and the more readily you can create your destiny.

So many of the changes we want to make, but cannot yet accomplish, are stymied because we have within us unexamined conflicting intentions. For example, part of our higher self may say we should change, but part of our lower self may say we should not. Unless this divergent intention is directly confronted, and resolved, this type of conflict tears us apart inside. Unless we have identified and scrutinized these conflicts, they will continue to wreak havoc in our lives.

A desired change can and will proceed when we have reached a place of inner alignment, when we have reconciled the previously conflicting places within us. That is not to say that all parts must be in enthusiastic support of a change. But it means that all the influential parts inside of us have been fully heard and considered. In the court of our own meditation, in a prayer session with God, there these parts can and should all be experienced, felt, considered, and evaluated. When we align our will with God's will, we can then judge which parts inside us we will allow to direct our lives. How our life unfolds from this point forward is a function of how much relative importance we attach to these different parts.

When we choose to support our higher self and its intention to unify all parts of our consciousness, our life will then unfold in an unimagined and miraculous way. For example, creativity can show up only in wholeness. To the extent that we compartmentalize our consciousness, we split off parts of our consciousness. In this splitting, we block our potential creativity. When we integrate, unify, and align all the parts within us, we will then be in a position to approach our challenge in a whole new way, in a vastly more empowered and creative manner. When we are in a state of inner unification, we will be in touch with the true reality of who we are, and we will become aware that everything can and does change.

Personal Story:
Milton was a big fan of metaphysical and esoteric literature. From sources in that domain, he had been playing with the notion that we each create our experience of reality, based on

the thoughts that we have. More recently he had been participating in an online discussion group, and one of the other men in that group had written that, "nobody really cares about you or your life, so you might as well live the life you want to live, rather than subscribe to social expectations." Milton liked the urging to live a life of choice, and for days these words ran around and around in his head. They had a profound effect on him because they played to part of his lower self. These words were in support of a misconception he had about life: that nobody cared about him, his feelings, or his needs. While he indeed had that experience as a child, part of his lower self held onto the belief that all the rest of his life was going to show up as more of the same.

As he walked to the post office to pick up his mail at lunchtime during a workweek, he was thinking about whether these words were true. He wondered whether anybody genuinely cared about him or his life. Sure, there were other people in his life; for example, he had a girlfriend and other personal friends too. But maybe they were just hanging around because they wanted some things from him. Maybe they didn't really care about him or his life. When he got to the post office, he saw two government employees whom he knew because he had repeatedly done business with them. He said hello, and they greeted him cordially using his name. He wondered whether they really cared about him and his life. He thought not. Probably their polite responses were just a part of their job description.

As he was walking back to his office, he remembered the notion that his thoughts created his experience. He had been pleased the previous day when he had entertained the thoughts that he was competent and resourceful. That positive self-talk had supported him in successfully accomplishing a painting project about which at first he had serious doubts (he had feared he would be spilling paint in irreparable and conspicuous places). During his walk, Milton wondered whether his thoughts about other people caring were setting him up for an experience of separation and loneliness. He then chose to align with his higher self, which intended that he have an experience of loving connection with others.

At that point in the walk, Milton crossed paths with a neighbor whom he knew, a man called Peter, who was accompanied by a woman Milton didn't know. Milton said hello in a polite but not too friendly manner. He expected the other two would simply say hello and continue walking, but they stopped and apparently wanted to talk. The woman asked him whether his name was Milton. He replied that it was, feeling surprised that she cared enough to ask.

The woman went on to ask Milton whether he grew up in a particular large industrial city, a city more than three thousand miles away from where the conversation was taking place. Indeed, Milton had grown up in that city, and the woman was correct about not just this fact, but a variety of other personal details of Milton's life as a child. Milton was quite surprised that this woman knew so much about him, because he had not shared such details with Peter, and so Peter could not have gone on to share those details with the woman.

In general, as a policy, Milton did not share personal information about his life as a child with either his personal friends or business associates, because he considered these details to be irrelevant and distracting. Since he couldn't understand how this woman knew about him, for Milton, the conversation was getting quite interesting. The woman then asked him whether as a child he lived next to the Renners, a family that lived on Allen's Lane. Milton replied that indeed he had. At this point, Milton was wondering if he was being set-up by a court process server, or some bizarre police sting operation. The whole conversation was getting unbelievable, and Milton wondered how she could have come to know about him, and why she was asking these questions.

The woman then asked whether Milton went to a certain small high school, and to that he also replied affirmatively. She indicated that she too went to that high school, and was in the class just behind his. Milton asked for her name because he didn't remember anybody who looked like her. She gave her full name. Milton vaguely remembered who she was, but he would never have recognized her on the street, because it had after all been forty years since his graduation. Since he graduated, Milton had never attended any school reunions or other school functions, because he lived so far away, so his inability to recognize this woman was not surprising. Evidently she had a crush on Milton many years ago, and he never knew about it, that is until this conversation took place.

The woman went on to say that she remembered his face, after all of these years. She had thought that it was indeed Milton, but because he now wore a short beard, she wanted to check her hunch out with him. Milton was flabbergasted, especially because he didn't have any sort of a relationship with her back then. To the best of his recollection, all he knew about her was that he had read her name on a class roster at the time of his graduation.

He gave her his business card and they all said their good-byes. On the remainder of his walk, Milton thought it was miraculous that his shift in thought patterns—his considering that people genuinely cared about him and his life—would prompt such an immediate response from the spirit world. In his aligning his intentions with truth, in his choosing to live according to the intentions of his higher self, Milton discovered that people genuinely cared about him and his life ... at least some people did.

Journal Questions:

(1) To do this exercise you will need to find a place of relative calm and quiet. Listen into yourself, and identify the predominant feeling of this moment. What thoughts go along with this feeling? Are these thoughts and feelings in alignment with your conscious intentions?

(2) Are you genuinely open to accepting whatever you may find in your self-search? Is there a certain place that is off-limits? If so, what is that place, and why can you not be fluid and flexible, going to that place like any other?

(3) Are there two separate domains of your consciousness that you consider to be irreconcilable? For instance, could you be in touch with both your sexuality and your spirituality at the same time? If there are two irreconcilable parts within you, why are they not possible to align, unify, and combine?

29

Revealing the Positive and Constructive Inside You

Affirmation:

I HONOR MY life as a process of spiritual growth. I acknowledge that part of my great task on earth is to transform certain parts of my consciousness, so that they may once again be positive and constructive.

Core Idea:

All human beings create their experience on earth based on their thoughts. Thoughts include beliefs, perspectives, ideas, and feelings (consider the possibility that feelings are simply unthought thoughts). To the extent that these causal thoughts are positive and constructive in their orientation, to that same degree will the experience of an individual be joyous, loving, expansive, meaningful, and rewarding. To the extent that these causal thoughts are negative and out of truth, to that same degree will they bring about experiences of pain, difficulty, and trouble. The task for us is thus to free ourselves from negativity and untruth, so that our true nature can be experienced and revealed. Underneath this negativity and untruth, we will find our inherent nature, which is divine substance.

A great many of us blow the good-versus-evil story way out of proportion. When we overcome our dualistic thinking (which says things are either good or bad, black or white, night or day, etc.), then there is only good. When we overcome our destructiveness and errors about reality, when we heal the straying parts of our consciousness, then we come back to the realization that there is only the positive. The negative and unevolved aspects of ourselves are thus like a cloud that obscures the sun. Through our own personal work we dissipate the cloud so that the sun behind it (God's presence, truth, love, beauty, joy, and other positive life indicators) can shine through. Ultimately there is no fight between the forces of good and the forces of evil; there is only a fight between those that know God and those who do not yet know Him. There is no force of evil per se, there are only people who are separated from and alienated from God.

A human being who knows that his own fate is a function of personally generated consciousness is thus in a position to make a significant change. But a person who does not believe that his fate is a function of consciousness remains disempowered. To the extent that someone acknowledges that he can change, to that extent is he able to make a conscious choice to give up negativity and untruth. Those who do not believe that they can change will continue to blame external circumstances for their unhappiness and suffering. And those who do not believe they can change, with their disempowering viewpoints, will indeed go on to create the undesirable circumstances about which they complain. The psychologists call this process of self-hypnosis a "self-fulfilling prophesy."

So underneath the lower self, the childish ways, the unevolved aspects of our consciousness, is the divine self. The latter already exists, and is therefore effortless. Giving up negativity and untruth does not place an individual in a dangerous and shaky position in which the positive and constructive must then be generated from scratch. Giving up negativity and untruth will simply reveal the positive and constructive parts of the self that already exist. These parts can unfold, be revealed, and expand when a human being allows them to come forward, because he or she has done the personal work required. When a person has removed the blocks (negativity and untruth) to this experience (that all life is good), these blocks will no longer stand in the way of making the change that we wish to bring about in the world or within ourselves.

Personal Story:

Lionel was a young high-tech workaholic with a compulsive and obsessive personality. Whatever he did, he did it one hundred percent, and then he would go back over it again, just to make sure he did it right. Often the going-back-over-things process would repeat several times. It is not surprising that, given his extraordinary level of effort and focus, Lionel frequently would work on a project for twelve hours straight without eating. He would often put in fifteen- or sixteen-hour days, and then fall asleep after midnight because he was exhausted. The next morning he would wake-up early and promptly go right back into the same process, repeating it day after day.

If he wasn't working, Lionel would obsess about his house, how everything looked, how everything was arranged, and whether it was clean enough. If he wasn't working or obsessing about his house, he would be focused intensely on his garden. Regarding his garden, he would worry about insect infestations, invasive plants, whether certain plants had the right soil chemistry to thrive, etc. Although he was able to constructively channel this worrying, burdensome, and intense personality trait into the world of business, and make some good money, this way of approaching life was exhausting. There was very little space in his life for other people, including his girlfriend. There was also very little space in his life just to be himself, and just to feel his real feelings.

With the aid of a therapist, Lionel discovered a part of himself that was terrified of his feelings, particularly his feelings of being dominated, controlled, and abused by his long-deceased and violent grandfather. He was terrified of once again experiencing the helplessness, powerlessness, and sense of life being out of control, which he knew only too well as a child. He came to understand that his obsessive and compulsive personality traits acted as a defensive shield, blocking him from feeling these feared feelings. As long as he intensely preoccupied himself with matters out there in the world, he could temporarily push these scary feelings out of his awareness.

His therapist encouraged Lionel to re-experience these feelings, to go through them repeatedly, each time a bit more deeply, intensely, and completely. In his daily life, Lionel took up meditation, as a way to allow these feelings to organically come to the surface of his consciousness. He made deliberate efforts to create unscheduled space in his life where he could feel these feelings, especially the ones that had long been held at bay. When he tapped into them, he was reassured and comforted by the notion that beneath them was his divinely connected self, the part that was connected to God. Even though he was often emotionally activated or upset when he connected with his feelings, Lionel was still able to pray to know his true nature, that place of constructiveness and posi- tivity, that place of truth, wisdom, love, and strength. This approach fortified him, and allowed him to rapidly proceed to become a more rounded and balanced human being.

These days Lionel is still a computer programmer, an area where his compulsiveness and dedication to exquisite detail has paid off. But he goes about doing his work in an entirely different manner than he did before. Rather than being a workaholic, he mixes in a lot of physical exercise with his work. Rather than simply focusing on a problem for hour after hour, often day after day, he now shifts gears often, repeatedly asks for inspiration, and takes a lot of breaks. Innovative and successful ways to write computer programs come to him through his meditation and during the many breaks he takes during his new workdays. While his work is still of the highest caliber, the toll that it takes on his body and his psyche is much reduced. His girlfriend is also delighted to note that Lionel is more of a relaxed and grounded person these days.

Journal Questions:

(1) If you were to let go of all blame, and stop pointing to external events as the source of your misery and pain, if you were to adopt the perspective that you create one hundred percent of your own inner experience, who do you think you would be then? Flesh this answer out with a multiple-sentence description of who you would be then.

(2) If you are connected with God, if you are a creation of God, then all divine powers are at your disposal (provided you are unified with your positive intention). When you clear away negativity and untruth, when you step into your divinely connected self, you will be able to create an entirely different experience in life. After reading

this, what part of you still argues for your victimhood and powerlessness? What part of you refuses to even consider this expansive possibility?

(3) As a thought experiment, consider that you were able to live your life with the notion that you were constructively and positively creating everything. Imagine that doing this is effortless, natural, and easy—because you are, after all, relying on something that already exists inside you—your divinely-connected self. Describe a particular scene in your current day-to-day life that has historically been accompanied by your negativity and your pain. Then look at this same scene again, only this time understand that you are constructively and positively creating everything. How would you be seeing the scene with that latter perspective, and what would be happening?

30

Allowing Yourself to Be Affected by Life

Affirmation:

LIFE IS INHERENTLY supportive and benign. I open my heart and allow myself to be touched by, and affected by all that is happening in and around me. I can navigate and learn from every thought, feeling, emotion, experience, and situation. I can handle whatever life brings me.

Core Idea:

On unconscious levels, and often on conscious levels as well, we think that having pain and being hurt is terrible, something we cannot handle. In these unexamined places within ourselves, we often have an excessive fear of these experiences, believing that they are something we must avoid at all costs. The reality of life is that there will be pain and hurt. There is no way to avoid it. If we relax and accept that difficult experiences are just part of life, something to go through, life becomes a whole lot less scary.

The fear of being hurt, of having emotional pain, for many people, takes on an irrational and illogical importance. It is as if they are afraid of death, and in order to avoid death, they commit suicide. The important and paradoxical point here is that the avoidance of pain and hurt, and the adoption of needless defenses against these experiences, actually causes additional pain and hurt. So through this avoidance, we go on to create pain and hurt, which we would not have had to go through had we been open to experiencing whatever life brought to us.

Pain and hurt are life's ways of getting our attention, are in fact our teachers. They force us to look at what we don't want to see. Pain and hurt need to be accepted and allowed to work their way through our psyches. To the extent that we push them away, to that same extent they stick around. It is ironic, but when we avoid and refuse to deal with our pain and hurt, these experiences remain with us longer than they would otherwise. If allowed to take their natural course, pain and hurt will change, like all experiences do. This is why many cultures recognize a period after people die, a period of mourning, a time set aside for us to go through our own inner process. The faster and more directly that we fully embrace our feelings and our inner experience, the faster we will learn from these things, and the faster we will move on to new experiences.

On an inner level, we often rebel against and object to both pain and hurt. Part of us childishly believes that they should not be part of our life. This part of us actually touches an aspect of the deeper long-term truth, which is that we need not be affected by our situation, by the circumstances of our life. In the long run, our happiness can be solely determined by ourselves, and can be a reflection of the successful inner work that we have done. But this is an advanced state of consciousness, a state that is rare in this world. Our egos misinterpret this possibility, this sense of where we are going, thinking that there must be something terribly wrong with us, or with our life, if we are now experiencing pain and hurt. For this moment, given the level of consciousness that the vast majority of us have, we can expect that there will be pain and hurt. This is because we have caused that pain and hurt, and it is up to us to take self-responsibility for what we have created, to heal these places where we have been in error and therefore also where we have been needlessly destructive.

If we define suffering as holding on to our pain and hurt, then our suffering is a measure of our imperfection. In that part of our life where we are suffering most, that is precisely where we are most needing to do some inner work. If we can focus on that specific area, then we can reorient and reeducate those parts that are in error and destructiveness, and thus we purify our psyches. If we can shift our consciousness in this way, by zooming-in on the part where we are suffering most, then the hurt and pain will likewise be rapidly healed.

This takes work, and certainly will not happen overnight. This process takes a while because human beings are complicated creatures, and the strings (the causes of our pain and hurt) have become twisted and knotted up in a big ball, somewhat like the mythical Gordian knot. This Gordian knot, representing the problems in our life, seems at first to be insolvable. But it is possible to untie the strings, to unravel the knot, to relax our defenses, and to clarify the true causes and effects. This noble task is not achieved easily, but it is absolutely worth the time and diligence that we put into the effort.

One of the most important strategies for unraveling the Gordian knot of our pain and hurt, for untangling and unraveling where we have become all tied up inside, is relaxation and acceptance. The more relaxed and accepting we become, the more objective we can be about our pain and hurt. The more objective we can be, the more new options and new possibilities will occur to us. The more objective we can be, the more we can see the long-term consequences of our fear of being hurt and having pain. In this objective place we can also understand how we needlessly create pain and hurt for ourselves, and others too, and how we can stop doing that. The more we can then relax and accept our situation, the more we are willing to look at it honestly and completely, the faster will we be able to begin to change things for the better.

This relaxation and acceptance of pain and hurt does not involve a hopeless masochism, which would only perpetuate pain and hurt. Nor does this relaxation and acceptance involve a cringing revolt against what life has brought us, because we acknowledge that—in keeping with the notion of karma—we have on some level brought on these experiences. Instead, if we can embrace the truth of our lives in this moment, if we can go through the pain and the hurt, if we can learn from what life is teaching us, then these experiences will be transformed into pleasure and joy. It is a paradox, but we cannot obtain pleasure and joy unless we are willing to experience pain and hurt. We cannot transform our experience of pain and hurt unless we completely know and understand how it has come into our lives, and how we have in some way contributed to its manifestation.

Personal Story:

Penelope was the third of four girls in a traditional family that was always having serious trouble with money. Both her mother and her father worked full-time, even though the house contained four young children. To look after the young girls, Penelope's maternal grandmother would often stay overnight at the house and run the household.

When Penelope was six, her mother contracted a very aggressive type of breast cancer. This meant that her mother was often away from the house, staying in the hospital, getting chemotherapy treatments, going through medical tests, and meeting with doctors. After her mother was diagnosed with cancer, money became even tighter than it had been before, because one of the breadwinners was out of commission. Because she was going through her own shock of the diagnosis, all of a sudden Penelope's mother became largely unavailable emotionally. The family members were all freaked out about the possibility that Penelope's mother might soon die, and their unspoken upset seemed to play off other family members' comparable feelings, much like a pinball machine racking-up lots of points. Nobody knew what to do, and the emotional air in the house was one of great tension and worry.

Being of Scandinavian descent, the family did not talk much about their emotions. That lack of emotional communication at this tense time her life, made Penelope still more upset and worried. As might be expected, the young girls began acting out, and Penelope's grandmother didn't know how to control them. In a desperate effort to get Penelope to comply with her rules and do the assigned chores, her grandmother told Penelope that it was because she was a bad girl that her mother had come down with cancer.

To an adult such a statement would be nonsensical, but to an impressionable and upset young girl, a girl with a still-forming sense of logic, the thought that Penelope was personally responsible for her mother's cancer was horrible and scary. Because these things weren't discussed in the house, and because her mother was then emotionally unavailable to reality-test this assignment of blame, the statement went unchallenged for years, and it later became part of Penelope's unconscious defense structure, her strategy for dealing with life.

As a result, Penelope believed that she was responsible for the sickness and subsequent deaths of the people around her. Even though she was now forty-five years old, she still harbored the belief that she was responsible for her deceased mother's cancer. Still using this same child logic, Penelope also believed she was responsible for her late husband's kidney cancer and death. She also had a few friends who had gotten sick and died, and she irrationally believed that somehow she must additionally be the cause of their health problems and deaths. In this regard, she believed she must have a curse or a hex placed on her. On one level she did, although she didn't acknowledge that it was her own mind that had adopted this personal superstition.

In a new romantic relationship with a man, Penelope was confronted by her new boyfriend about how she held on persistently to the childhood twisted logic that supported her unreasonable feelings of responsibility for the sicknesses and deaths of others around her. She took his confrontation to sessions with her therapist, and through these sessions Penelope came to appreciate that there was no logical linkage between being "good" and the health of those around her.

Penelope's inner work revealed how she had, from the time she was six, demanded a perfectionist standard of herself. Since the time that she was accused by her grandmother, Penelope was clear that she had better never be a "bad girl," lest she then cause serious health problems for other people. She had since then been a diligent rule upholder, always doing the right thing, and never questioning the rules for fear that even the questioning would be considered "bad." On one level she now saw how she could not possibly have that much power over the health of others. For Penelope to be able to dictate the health and life span of people around her would be a total denial of both the will and the choices of those people.

This impossible-to-obtain standard, to always be "good," often made Penelope unhappy because those close to her would inevitably have health problems. Penelope would then take these manifestations as proof that in some way she wasn't being a good girl. Even though Penelope was an intelligent woman, based on this erroneous unconscious belief, it was then time for her to redouble her efforts, and to work harder at being good. That extra effort only exhausted her. When she saw how this perfectionist ideal was making her unhappy, she let go of it, and so gained a great deal of new inner freedom. Fortunately, she understood this more truthful perspective before her neurosis damaged her own health.

Journal Questions:

(1) How do you hold yourself back in life, in an attempt to avoid having a particular experience of hurt and pain? Specifically what is your defense strategy here?

(2) Exactly what is the hurt and pain that you believe you must not experience? Being honest and objective, what in reality would happen if you were to experience that hurt and pain?

(3) How have you unwittingly caused yourself needless hurt and pain? Said differently, how have you paradoxically caused yourself needless trouble, because you have resisted this same hurt and pain?

31

Learning the Lesson That Frustration Brings

Affirmation:

IF THIS EXPERIENCE is painful or undesirable, I can nonetheless trust it, I can bear the feelings it brings, I can relax into it, and I can make the best of it. Perhaps this experience is not as catastrophic as I have up until now believed. Perhaps something good can come of it.

Core Idea:

Based on our history and our personal issues, we all color reality in our own personal ways. We are all, on some levels of our personality, subjective and out of touch with reality. This place of subjectivity is the road into the resolution of the problem that we face.

One relevant characteristic of a true leader is impartiality and objectivity. A true leader can also admit in what ways she is not impartial and objective. By admitting bias and subjectivity, a true leader comes back to impartiality and objectivity. The most important arena in which to embrace this aspect of true leadership is in our relationship with own psyches. To the extent that we can inhabit this impartiality and objectivity viewpoint with our own psyches, then we will also be able to do the same thing out in the world at a later time.

Another relevant aspect of leadership is the willingness to bear frustration. The child inside each of us wants to have her way, right now, exactly the way she wants it, and from everybody. This demanding attitude may at first sound unbelievable, but if you honestly look for this child within, you will no doubt find him or her. Even considering the possibility that such a child lurks within—that thought alone will often bring up denial, evasion, and resistance. This part of us knows that if we honestly admitted the existence of this inner child, then we would most likely need to change. And the child within does not like to change, so it is not surprising that it denies, evades, and resists. If we don't go beyond that initial response, we forfeit the opportunity of walking the road to resolving the serious problem with which we are wrestling.

Our inner child is angry because the world is not showing up in the way she demands. She does not want to wait for the world to conform to her demands. The child does not maturely understand the nature of time, nor does she understand that all things will change. If this situation that you confront is painful and difficult, the child within believes that it will always be that way. We all need to consider that the inner child has an erroneous view of the world, and she would cease to be angry if she understood and accepted how the world actually works.

This tyrannical child can run our lives if we allow her to do so. A true leader is able to step into an objective and impartial adult place, where the child within can be seen clearly, and then with a loving engagement, discipline the child as the circumstances require. Punishment is not required or advisable. Discipline in this case simply means setting and maintaining limits on the influence of the tyrannical inner child. Discipline involves the willingness to simply be with the situation, not to push for instant gratification, while at the same time realistically knowing that such instant gratification cannot be obtained at this point.

The key to unraveling this difficulty with the child within lies in overcoming the perceived duality found in the painful or difficult situation we face. On one level we grab at something, and then on another level we push that something away. We are simultaneously saying that we "must have it," and also saying we "must not have it." This tense and painful state can only be overcome when we are objective and impartial, when the adult in us clearly sees the duality. Then the adult can note that the child has one or more erroneous viewpoints that claim we must simultaneously have two mutually exclusive things. Of course the world is not going to oblige, it will not deliver two mutually exclusive things, so in this place we experience frustration. Anxiety is thus fostered by the child's belief that she must have something that cannot be.

So the investigation into what this frustration has to teach us will eventually help us transcend both pain and difficulty. Every frustration has some liberating and valuable lesson behind it. By considering this possibility, we open a door previously closed to us. In most instances, we have been so focused on battling against the frustration that we hadn't even considered the possibility that life was seeking to teach us something important. The more we resist and battle against the frustration, the more rigid and positional we become. The more rigid and positional we are, the more do we block the door that could readily open for us.

Although being overwhelmed with a frustration may provide a break, and then chance to adopt a new perspective, it is far better to proactively and courageously explore the meaning behind the frustration that we face. So we need to knock on the door of our higher self here, we need to call on our inner guidance, and we need to ask it what this frustration has to teach us. If we do that, we will be astounded to discover how this frustration is in fact our friend and teacher, not the enemy and undesirable menace that we imagined.

Personal Story:

Having recently recovered from a serious long-term illness, Peter was looking for a new career. In an effort to get a sense for what it might be like to be a professional mediator, Peter had gone to mediation school. He was originally thinking that it might be both fun and lucrative to be a mediator. He was attracted to the honesty, conflict resolution, and potential healing that were a part of this work. He even tried his hand with a few divorce mediations, and based on the feedback he received, the involved parties said that he had helped a great deal. Nonetheless, he turned away from mediation as a line of work because he felt it would be bad for his health to be regularly in the midst of such intense anger and blame. Here, as in several other aspects of his life, his inner conflict was revealed.

Peter also sat on the board of directors for the local water company in his rural community. During one board meeting, Peter was shocked at the intensity and acrimony of the yelling between two other board members, Harry and Jesse. Jesse was accusing Harry of dishonesty and covering up his mistakes related to a well that had been drilled some time back. Jesse was also upset because he took a joking side comment offered by Harry in a personal way, as an insult about the way he handled money. This particular board meeting had to be prematurely terminated because the yelling and threats got out of hand, and Harry exited the meeting. If Harry had not exited this meeting when he did, a fistfight was threatened to be next.

In the midst of this yelling at the board meeting, Peter felt frozen and unable to move, somewhat like a deer caught in the headlights of a speeding car. The yelling reminded him of how his mother had yelled at him when he was a child, how he wouldn't know what to do about it, and how he felt all locked-up inside. The child within felt he needed to exit the meeting to prevent physical violence. On another level he felt like he must stay, because the meeting was taking place in his house. Peter also felt like he had to stay because he was a trained mediator, and so he was supposed to not just be comfortable with conflict, but also supposed to be able to direct people constructively in the midst of such conflict.

Peter's inner conflict meant that he said little at the time of the yelling. All he could muster were the words, "let's investigate this to see what the truth is." In retrospect, he was disappointed in himself, disappointed that he had not taken on more of a leadership role at the time of the argument. Upon further reflection, he noted the conflict within himself, the place where he wanted to run away, and at the same time he wanted to stay, be a mediator, and bring peace to the situation. He discovered his fear that the dispute would escalate into physical violence, would cause members to resign from the board, or would cause a fistfight that then seriously damaged his house. From this inner place, Peter noted how he was primarily driven by fear, mostly the fear for his own physical safety. He saw that he was blocking his full experience of the event, holding back his own feelings, as well as an examination of what it all meant on a deeper level.

Peter curiously looked more deeply into the meaning of his frozenness, and of the frustration that he experienced. He was surprised to see the many ways in which he was constantly blocking what life was giving to him. For example, he often felt isolated from, and unknown by the other people who were regularly in his life. These experiences of isolation and separateness were in part caused by this same emotional blocking.

Delving more deeply into his personal experience, Peter noted that his blocking was preventing the best he had to offer from coming into the world. For example, his leadership and desire to give his best did not emerge in the midst of the dispute with the board. Likewise, he saw how this blocking prevented him from receiving what the world was offering him, in terms of friendship, love, and companionship.

Peter started to open to the possibility that his true security and protection lay with his openness to the truth, the giving up of his defenses, and his letting go of his hard and brittle walls. He saw how his reception of beauty, wisdom, and other insights were also dependent on a certain openness and inner flexibility, instead of on his continued defensiveness. So his first step was to bring down these walls within himself.

Peter then had a conversation with the chairman of the board, suggesting a mediation process involving both Harry and Jesse. Although they did not choose to work with him as a mediator, because he was a member of the board, and therefore not independent, they did soon thereafter get into mediation. Although the resolution was not the sought-after scenario (the matter was resolved by the resignation of one of the board members), Peter was in retrospect delighted that he had discovered how he had been blocking life, others, and his own feelings.

Journal Questions:

(1) What specifically is frustrating you about the situation you wish to change? What is your attitude about this frustration? Can you bear it? Is it unacceptable? Is it dangerous? Flush this out by revealing all your feelings and emotions about this frustration.

(2) About this experience of frustration, what are your intentions? Specifically, what are you grabbing for, and what are you pushing away? Are these intentions in any way incompatible? Are the intentions in any way inconsistent with reality?

(3) If you were to be objective and impartial, if you were to take full responsibility for your part in the situation that brings frustration, what would your assessment be? Have you been blinded by your own self-interest or self-righteousness? Have your resentments or demands prevented you from seeing the big picture? Have your feelings, like fear, guilt, jealousy, and competition, caused you to color the situation in an unfair and untrue way?

32

Moving with the Flow and No Longer Fighting with Life

Affirmation:

I EMBRACE ALL that is, and recognize it as a perfect out-picturing of various levels of consciousness. I accept and let in the truth of everything in my life. I go with the flow, and allow myself to be a part of the river of life—a river forever moving with the changes that need to happen, the changes that are, on some level, already underway.

Core Idea:

Resistance to what is true is futile and a waste of energy. If we insist on maintaining such resistance, it will only postpone the inevitable, waste energy, and cause destructive repercussions. If we let go of our resistance, and pay attention to what's actually happening around us, we will notice that each moment shows up differently, newly, and largely beyond our conscious control. Like a kaleidoscope, our inner experience is always different, always changing.

The changes that still need to take place in our lives, the changes that have not yet happened but are long overdue, are caused by our resistance to, and our pushing away of, the truths that we now need to embrace. To bring about a cure, a healing, and a necessary transformation, we will often need to go to the places inside ourselves that we most want to avoid.

Resistance and blocking of the natural flow, the way in which things keep changing inside us, that resistance and blocking occurs only because our ideas of who we are, or who we have to be, do not conform to reality. By denying the existence of the truth, we do not remove this truth. By making believe that we are someone different from whom we really are deep down inside—that masquerading will not empower us to create our sought-after reality.

When we block our inner experience by resisting the truth, we are playing the role of a child. Children do not fully understanding the truth, and society recognizes that fact, for example by denying them certain privileges that adults enjoy. For example, children are not permitted to drive automobiles because they are widely understood to lack the judgment, discretion, and self-control that an adult generally possesses. So when each of us is blocking the truth, we need to ask ourselves, "In this particular difficult situation, have I adopted the role of a child?"

Children will often deny the truth for silly, unjustified, or stubborn reasons. One way that this manifests is a refusal to go along with the truth, in the hope that the child might be able to thereby get his way. For example, a child may throw a tantrum because his parent doesn't buy him something (perhaps a toy) that the parent obviously cannot afford, something that the child has already been told he cannot have right now. In situations such as this, the child typically will have a disproportionate reaction, where he blows the little truth that he cannot have this thing right now way out of proportion. This is because the child only thinks in dualistic terms: good or bad, right or wrong, etc. Since this truth about not having the sought-after item feels bad, life must therefore be all must bad. Here the child is being not just selfish, but shortsighted as well, because at some point in the future, the child may in fact be able to have the sought-after item.

In such an example, and in many similar situations, the child refuses to consider the larger issues, such as the financial situation of the family, and what sacrifices by others might be required in order for the child to get what he wants. So too it is with personal work, where the child inside us would squash the desire to look at some relatively minor unpleasant aspect of the psyche, because to do so would seem to open the door to some horrible future, some Pandora's box of all bad things. Likewise, under these circumstances, the child is thinking only of himself, not seeing the larger situation, and how it is not the time to buy the sought-after item. If we can step into the larger truth of our long-term personal growth, then a moment of pain as we confront the reality of an unevolved part in ourselves, that will be resisted by the child, but the adult will see clearly that it is definitely in our long-run best interests to engage with this self-confrontation. Thus we can readily see that confronting a place of childishness in us is conducive to moving with, and learning from, the flow of life.

Some of us need to examine our unconscious conclusion that children seem to be better off than adults in this respect. On some level of our psyche, at some point in the past, many of us have unconsciously reached an erroneous conclusion, a conclusion that is definitely not conducive to the free flow of the river of life. For example, we may have concluded that a child's approach is to be preferred, because we want to be given what we need, just as children are given what they need. This limited perspective holds that children are not required to go out and obtain what they need by themselves, but can instead receive without having to stand on their own two feet. In reality, when we are adults, we are best advised not to make believe that we are still children in order to get what we need. So it is ill advised for us to create the helplessness, weakness, and passivity that this childish approach to life engenders, in the hope that what we need will then be given to us. As adults, we are competent to give to life by allowing the free movement of our inner experience, and by directly confronting the reality of that experience. It is through the self-responsibility inherent in the latter approach that we will more readily get what we need as adults.

For even the most evolved of us, there will be moments when we are in darkness, for example when we are gripped by the demanding child within. In these moments we are temporarily disconnected from God. It is only natural that at these times, in the midst of conflicts, problems, and apparent contradictions, we would have a dark mood. We need to know that these moments are only temporary, and that by embracing the truth of the moment, by learning from it, by allowing it, by going through it, by riding with it as though we were floating down the river of life, we actually speed its resolution. It is in the relaxing, and in requesting a reestablishment of a divine connection, that we will come back to knowing both the truth and the best course of action. And through that connection we can understand why things have been continuing in the present way, so that we can go on to make the change that is now required.

Personal Story:

Preston had a book in him, an idea that just wouldn't go away. In the shower, he got not only a clear idea for the book, but also a clear idea of about twenty chapter headings. This was incredible to him, because he had never experienced so much information all at once, like some download of important personal information coming from another place. Not bothering to dry off after the shower, he shivered and dripped all over the carpet while he wrote the ideas down. He was inspired, and excited about these new ideas, and he very much wanted to follow through and manifest the book idea that had sprung into his awareness without any warning or expectation.

Although he couldn't really explain it in a rational way, he felt as though it was his personal task to write this book. Nonetheless, he had other plans for his life, and this book idea decidedly did not fit in with those plans. Much to his consternation, in his regular meditations, he would keep getting new ideas to include in the book. He wrote all these ideas down, and after a period of trying to "move on" with his life, he once again kept feeling a gentle push to get on with writing the book.

Later, after about twelve months of trying to forget about this experience, he all at once realized that the research for the book would in many ways help him with his own life. It was only then that Preston was willing to try his hand at writing a few chapters. The chapters came easily, and the process flowed naturally, and to his surprise, he felt inexplicably guided on some level. He wrote a few more chapters, and they too came forward easily.

He kept pushing the book to the background of his daily schedule, feeling as though his work-for-pay, his charitable giving with people in need, and his family's personal demands on his time, were all more important than this book. He found himself being quite creative when it came to reasons why he shouldn't work on the book that he seemed called to write. In spite of this blocking, he was still able to fit in a little writing from time to time.

One day, much to his surprise, the first draft of the book was already done. It only needed light editing and a publisher. In spite of that fact, he sat on the project for another twenty-four more months. All the while, he kept feeling this gentle push to complete and publish the book. Unable to shake that feeling, he talked with his therapist about how he was conflicted. His therapist asked him directly what he was afraid of, what undesirable things he thought would happen if the book was to be published. It seemed like a good question, perhaps even an obvious question, but nonetheless a question that that Preston had been afraid to ask himself.

With the help of his therapist, Preston got to the bottom of it: he was afraid that if the book was published, people would ask him to do things he wouldn't be able to refuse. He feared that he would then be forced to do as they requested or demanded. This wise therapist asked why he couldn't say "no" to these requests for speeches, or consulting projects, or whatever. Preston provided many answers, but none of them made rational and grounded sense for an adult with Preston's position in the world. The answers were all reflections of Preston's childhood, a disempowered experience of a child who thought he had absolutely no say in the way that things would go in his household.

By confronting each of these fears, explicitly and one at a time, Preston was able to generate the self-confidence needed to complete editing the book, and then to publish it too.

In retrospect, Preston is delighted with all the additional opportunities that have come about because he was willing to push the envelope, willing to go through his fears, willing to see that his fears were only phantoms left over from the past. These days he is delighted that he took greater responsibility for constructively creating the life he wanted, rather than resisting what wanted to happen—what in fact was already happening in spite of his continued resistance.

Journal Questions:

(1) When you don't like, or worse, when you fear, your own feelings and attitudes, you block your own awareness of them. You then obstruct the stream of your inner reality, the stream that should take your feelings and emotions where they want to go. Where do you dam up your own inner experience? What feelings or attitudes do you keep blocking?

(2) By repressing these feelings and attitudes, by creating a dam to your inner flowing nature, you create collateral damage. This subsequent metaphorical flood, or said differently, the unintended side effects, may take the form of inexplicable outbursts, moments of rage unrelated to

the situation, or other illogical behaviors that seem out of character. What are these moments of collateral damage? By not going with what wants to move, what damage are you creating in your life? Also notice whether there is a something in particular that is precipitating these outbursts; notice whether there is a common denominator that occurs before all such events.

(3) Rather than fighting with life, rather than blocking the feelings and attitudes you have inside, what would it be like to take down the walls to experiencing these things? Rather than a violent and sudden event, such as a flood, what if you were to gradually and responsibly remove parts of the dam, and to then let your inner river flow? If you used adult self-responsibility to remove the obstructions to what now needs to flow, what would your life look like then?

33

Understanding That You and Life Are Inseparable

Affirmation:

WHATEVER IS GOING on in my life is a reflection of what is going on inside me. I choose now to gain control over my life by becoming aware of, and responsible for, my own inner process.

Core Idea:

Our lives don't lie. Our lives are perfect reflections, or projections, of our inner states. Some people erroneously claim that their lives are incomprehensible, confusing, and meaningless. These people are out of touch with the direct connection between their inner experience and the events and circumstances of their lives. They believe they are separate from life, that they have somehow been placed on this planet, and that have nothing to do with how their lives show up.

On a deeper level, there is no separation between our inner state and our experience of life. Regardless of our interpretations about the circumstances of our lives, life and each one of us is one. Life is the sum total of all of our attitudes and beliefs, all of our past actions and reactions, all of our traits, and all of our gifts. Life is the gestalt of our inner reality. When we see the correspondence between our inner and our outer realities, for example how destructive beliefs have created pain in our lives, then we start to take advantage of a great teaching tool. This tool gives us back the power to direct our lives, gives us a mechanism to create a whole different life experience.

We are not straws in the wind, blown this way and that, unable to control what's happening in our lives. We are actually able to totally remake our outside life experiences, provided that we are willing to honestly and faithfully do the inner work. When we embrace the connection between inner and outer reality, we no longer need to fear life. Then we can come out of illusion, out of disharmony, out of destructiveness, and out of a belief in our helplessness.

When we have achieved a confidence in ourselves, our abilities, our talents, and our potentials, then we will also have achieved that same confidence in life. When we have gotten to know our inner reality, and have thoroughly explored it, we will have discovered that it's not as scary as we had feared it would be. When we come to know the dark recesses of our consciousness, then we realize that we need not be terrified of the influence that these aspects have over us. When we explore these different aspects of our consciousness, and can accept them and work with them, then we are able to decide that we are no longer willing to allow certain of them to run our lives.

Everyone's life has setbacks, defeats, and problems. When we have confidence in ourselves, confidence that we can meet and deal with every aspect of our inner world, then we are empowered to deal with those parts of our life experience that are not to our liking. We can then be willing to relinquish, to let go, to give over to the truth, and see that it is not a catastrophe that we did not get our way. We can then examine ourselves, and look for the ways in which we were participants in the creation of circumstances that we now find distasteful and/or undesirable.

To gain a new level of control over our lives, we must think about and deeply investigate our difficulties, the issues that we keep wrestling with, and those things that keep plaguing us. What if, as the law of karma says, we have helped to create these circumstances, either in this life, or in a prior life? Whether or not we believe in the existence of prior lives, if we can discover the seed inside each of us that has grown into our current life circumstances, then we have put our hands on the knobs and dials that control our current life experiences.

What if our fear of undesirable aspects in ourselves was simply an illusion? What if there were no parts of us—no matter how destructive, undesirable, or ugly—that needed to be rejected or pushed away? What if they were all, in the ultimate analysis, simply different aspects of the divine consciousness? Many of these aspects have lost their way, have become twisted, are in darkness, and are operating with misconceptions and distorted views of reality. Even though they may be twisted and distorted, they can still be converted back to their original nature. If we consider the possibility that there is nothing to fear within ourselves, nothing that we need to turn away from, nothing in us that cannot be healed, then we can relax with all of who we are today.

If who we really are on one hand, and what life really is on the other hand, are one and the same, and if we ceased to be afraid of any part of ourselves, then we would cease to be afraid of any part of life. In other words, we fear life, and others, to the same extent that we fear ourselves. We actually cannot fear anything if we no longer keep a secret part of ourselves from ourselves. If we enter the place where we have been hiding this secret part of ourselves, if we are willing to discover all that it entails, then we overcome self-alienation. Then we also—as a byproduct of this work—overcome our alienation from life.

Personal Story:

Brian was a brilliant middle-aged man who felt trapped by his circumstances, particularly the fact that he was the only breadwinner for his family with young children. He yearned to make what he considered a contribution in a bigger arena, notably to in some way be part of the government of his country. He felt a call to get involved in politics, but he couldn't define exactly what it was he should do. He felt cursed because he had such difficulty trying to specifically define what his contribution might be, and how he should move forward at that point in time. On the surface, definition of a personal career plan seemed to him such a simple thing to do. Yet he felt inexplicably blocked, and therefore unable to do anything constructive in this realm. His first step was to realize that having dreams of another work situation didn't mean that he was being disloyal to his family, and also that if he made a career change that he wouldn't necessarily become a failure in his role as the sole breadwinner. Once he saw those two things clearly, he was able to relax a bit and go deeper with his self-investigation.

Brian had six hand-written notebooks full of ideas that were new, practical, and important, and those notebooks contained innovative ideas that could realistically be used to upgrade the government in his country. He had talent and a contribution to make—that was not the issue. What he was missing was the willingness to honestly go deep inside of himself, to discover all of his intentions, and all the reasons why he wanted to get involved in politics. When he deeply investigated his intentions, he discovered a desire to exact revenge against his former classmates in graduate business school. Many of these classmates were then working in that country's government, and were openly critical of him because he did not choose their political career path. They belittled him for not attaining the same career success heights that they had achieved. Earlier in his process work, Brian had not wanted to see that part of his desire to be involved in politics was to show his old classmates that they were wrong about him. At this point, he felt some relief in his acknowledgment of this truth.

Every human being has a mixture of higher-self motives and lower-self motives. To make believe that we have only higher-self motives sets us up to be unhappy, because we clearly cannot live up to that requirement. Nonetheless, this is exactly what Brian was doing. He was insisting that his motives be perfectly clean and pure, and he didn't want to admit that he might have ulterior motives for his work in politics. This blocking meant that he didn't want to look at his lower-self motives. Because he refused to examine all of his intentions, he was unable to reach a place of inner alignment regarding his proposed political career. Without this inner alignment of his intentions, he would not allow himself to clarify the next steps in a new government-related career.

With the aid of his business coach, Brian made extensive lists of all of his motives, and these lists were made alternatively coming from both his higher-self and his lower-self. Through this process, he came to see that there was nothing within himself that needed to be feared. Although he still had work to do to purify and reeducate his lower-self aspects (such as the part that wanted revenge), he could be with all of these aspects, acknowledge them, and choose to not allow them to run his life. Brian came to see how incredibly unrealistic he had been, in this case insisting that he be perfectly holy and positively intentioned. He also came to see that this insistence to be only good was in fact blocking him from moving forward with his career development.

Through the examination of all of his motives for moving into a political career, as well as challenging those of them that were out of touch with reality, he was able to relax those inner areas that had been in conflict. He was then also able to relax in regard to his outer circumstances. Instead of leaving his family, which had previously seemed to be the only way to achieve this new career in government, he now imagined innovative ways that he could have his family life and his new political career at the same time. He also came to see that just because he had some lower-self motives to go into a political career, that didn't mean that he should give up on these new career goals. His relaxation also extended to an acceptance that, like all people, he had a mixture of both higher-self motives and lower-self motives, and that there was nothing to be ashamed of about that. The next steps in the manifestation of his dream then clearly came into focus, in part because he was no longer afraid of looking at certain dark parts within himself.

Journal Questions:

(1) Do you have a vague sense of hiding something inside yourself? Describe these feelings and thoughts. Why do you believe that you must keep this aspect of yourself under wraps? Can you at least be honest and open with yourself about this part?

(2) Specifically, what aspect of yourself do you believe you must keep in secret? Name it in clear terms. Honestly now, is it really as terrible as you had feared it would be?

(3) How would the unwillingness to look at and deal with this aspect within yourself manifest out there in the world? What undesirable or troublesome result might be created by your refusal to look at and deal with this aspect?

34

Challenging Misconceptions about Truth

Affirmation:

I LET GO of all preconceived notions about the truth, and seek to discover and experience the deeper, all-encompassing truth of this moment. I am open to any eventuality, even if it challenges what I have come to believe was the truth.

Core Idea:

There is only one ultimate bottom-line truth. The true facts take a particular form and a particular gestalt in this moment. They will change, but in this moment, the truth takes this one particular form. Everything in the world, in the universe, is changing. Thus there is no one forever-static truth except that: God exists, God is everywhere, and the universe operates by divine law. Outside of that, what was true yesterday may no longer be true today.

When our views of the world are static, stagnant, and unchanging, we inevitably create conflict, crisis, and upset. This is because our views, even if they were consistent with truth some time ago, may no longer be synchronized with the truth. In more cases than many of us care to admit, the truth has moved on, but our views of the world have not. For instance, we may have formed an over-generalized conclusion about life from childhood, such as "life is hard and difficult." As an adult, we may still be holding on to that belief, and thereby causing trouble for ourselves. Everything is moving, changing, vibrating, and transforming, and our views of the world must be doing the same—that is if we are going to live a life of harmony and peace.

The human experience, even for those who are enlightened and quite mature, involves seeing only a part of the larger, all-encompassing truth. Some people are better at getting a sense for the big picture, while other people excel at clearly seeing certain aspects of this larger truth. On a deeper level, what a person sees can be part of the truth, but it might at the same time be an apparent contradiction to some part of the truth that someone else sees. From the vantage point of this all-encompassing truth, there may be no contradiction, there may only be different people with different pieces of the puzzle. This is illustrated by an ancient Indian apocryphal story about several blind men, who had each experienced a single contact with only one part of an elephant. From their own personal and limited experience, each blind man thought he knew what an elephant was like. The blind man that contacted the trunk thought an elephant was long and flexible like a snake, the blind man that contacted a tusk thought an elephant was hard and smooth like a China plate, etc. As is the case with an elephant, the wider objective truth was much larger than any of these blind men knew. On the other hand, a man with sight can see the whole elephant, and so inform the blind men that they have only a part of the truth.

A wider and larger absolute truth does exist. The resolution of our problems is to be found via our efforts to know that larger absolute truth. We do not need to turn away from this investigation into absolute truth with a misguided conclusion that humans can only know the relative truth. By the relative truth, here we are referring to the subjective truth, that part of the truth that one person sees based on his own personal concepts and filters. These defeatist discussions about relative truth relegate truth to a position of personal taste or personal opinion. Discussions about relative truth propose that each of us can observe only a subjective personal truth. To the contrary, truth is not a matter of human preference, imagination, or illusion.

To claim that we can know only the relative truth is to adopt a viewpoint that plays a needlessly small game. This small game assumes that we are nothing but our separated ego-selves, that we do not have contact with God. People become disempowered because they think the relative truth is the end of the story, and in so doing, they miss the powerful opportunity of aligning with God's larger and all-encompassing truth.

To reach a place of inner unity, a place where we have a positive and constructive engagement with life, we must not be seduced by these relative truth arguments. We must not stop our personal search for the objective truth, the larger all-encompassing truth. If we don't believe that such a larger all-encompassing truth exists, of course then we create a self-fulfilling prophecy, and we will not be able to sense that larger truth.

Every one of us can see part of God's all-encompassing truth, but this opening does not manifest unless we believe it is possible. There is a spiritual truth, an all-encompassing wider and deeper truth, and it is important that people search for that ultimate objective truth through a process of self-discovery and self-knowing. It is also important that we ask for divine assistance so that we might be shown this larger all-encompassing wider truth.

For example, those who blindly follow a specific dogma, without thinking about whether it is true, without challenging it, these people are in compliance. Unless they shift their perspective, they will never have the personal experience of recognizing this all-encompassing wider truth. Similarly, those who define the truth as what others say it is are in consensus, but they too deny themselves the possibility of contacting the deeper all-encompassing truth. Likewise, intellectuals who throw all notions of the truth into one big bucket, labeling it all as subjective and relative truth, they too will deny themselves the possibility of experiencing this larger all-encompassing truth. Only through the door within ourselves, the door that leads to God, only through that door can we find the larger, objective, all-encompassing truth.

God and God's laws of the universe provide the ultimate truth. Everybody wants to know that larger truth, and everybody wants to go back to God, whether or not they admit it consciously and whether or not they admit it publicly. If we seek it, each one of us will receive that part of the larger truth that we are ready to deal with and assimilate at this point in our personal development. To expand our capacity to know the truth, we must knock on that door that opens the way back to God, we must ask for help in our efforts to know the ultimate objective all-encompassing truth.

Understanding and deeper insight will come as our openness to this possibility, and as our openness to this reality about truth, expands. If we are open to any eventuality, if we are willing to drop all of our preconceived ideas, if we are open to honestly and sincerely experiencing the all-encompassing deeper truth, whatever it may be, then we will be shown that deeper transcendent spiritual truth by God and his helpers.

Personal Story:

Horatio was an automobile engineer, a man well trained in the ways of logical thinking. For his whole career, he had worked in a big city, and he owned a house nearby. He had recently reached retirement age, and had stopped working. As much as he appreciated the big city, with his group of friends and family nearby, he yearned to move to the remote country. He wanted to get more grounded with nature, and live in a small community with a slower pace.

There was one particular small town about three hours north —a beautiful town right by the sea—that Horatio had visited many times on three-day-long weekends. To that place he felt inexplicably drawn. He dreamt that one day he would live there. But he hesitated.

Moving at his advanced age made no sense, or at least that's what he told himself. Every business he knew, everyone he knew, and even his own personal identity—were all tied up with this big city. At his age, to start over seemed like an insurmountable task. Reestablishing a new community seemed like an invitation to being lonely for many years, especially since he was divorced and had no girlfriend. The hassle associated with moving seemed overwhelming, and Horatio wondered how he would get the energy to go through with such a transition.

He went back and forth on this topic a great deal. Some days he was convinced he was going to move, but other days he was not. He vacillated so much that he made one of his good friends angry because he spoke so often about this decision, yet he didn't do anything about it. His friend's anger was a wake-up call, and

Horatio realized that his approach to this decision wasn't working. Horatio was in a vicious circle of repeatedly dreaming this dream, and then disempowering himself because he believed the dream was beyond his reach.

Horatio went over and over his thoughts and feelings, trying to determine what was true, and what was not. He made lists of the pros and cons of moving, he ranked his personal priorities, he listed the relative benefits of different locations, but all of this was still at the level of mind. Horatio then realized that he needed more insight, and that he needed to come to a deeper and more encompassing truth. He then decided to "turn it over to God." He prayed for guidance, and then was open to receiving a new level of guidance, and open to receiving an answer whatever that happened to be.

With this approach, after a few weeks, Horatio came to appreciate that he clearly did want to move away from the polluted, busy, noisy, pushy, high-pressure, expensive city where he had been working. But he didn't know where he would go. Trusting his guidance, he sold his house in the big city, and rented an apartment on a month-to-month basis in the suburbs. He gave himself all the time he needed, and this allowed him to be with the process as it unfolded. Traveling to different locations, he sampled what it was like to stay there. He stayed in the apartment for a year and a half, but then one day, he felt in his bones that it was time to move. Within two months, he had bought a house in, and completely moved to, his favorite rural town by the sea.

Since then, Horatio's life in this rural town has become a beautiful opening, a beautiful opportunity to recreate his life again. Moving gave him a chance to create a new lifestyle that was compatible with his current values, not those of his working life. Moving gave him a chance to create a new circle of friends who shared his interests and passions, not just a circle of friends who happened to work at the same organization. These days Horatio feels deep in his heart that his move was right, and he is glad that he gave himself the space of not knowing, the space of allowing himself to simply be in process, combined with the space of turning the decision over to God. He has since then also become impressed with the power of admitting what the mind can do, and what it cannot do, and he no longer feels the need to make believe that the mind is so powerful and all knowing.

Journal Questions:

(1) Only you can know your personal truth, and how the ultimate, objective, all-encompassing truth applies to your life. Other people cannot know this for you. In what ways have you believed the truth is based on some sort of consensus among people? In what part(s) of your life, especially in the area of the change that you seek to make, have you sold out to, and endorsed, the "truth" derived from the consensus of others?

(2) Many people say the "truth" is what conforms to their belief system. They claim all sorts of things are the "truth," but these people have no personal experience of these things. Some go so far as to say that these things that they don't know are "unquestionable." But this is not the truth; this is dogma. In what areas of your life, particularly in those related to the change that you seek to make, is the "truth" you have been using simply dogma?

(3) What would happen if you were to surrender yourself to, if you were to fully embrace, the deeper and all-encompassing truth? Do you fear that you would lose some outer freedom and/or some advantage? In what ways might you be placing your outer freedom and/or personal advantage above God's truth?

35

Embracing Yourself as an
Imperfect Human Being

Affirmation:

A S A HUMAN being I acknowledge that I still have work to do on myself, that I am not yet perfect. Although I know that demanding perfection would be counterproductive, I resolve to give my best to whatever life brings me.

Core Idea:

All human beings have places inside them that manifest hostility, destructiveness, cruelty, and selfishness. Likewise, we all harbor negative feelings and attitudes such as pride, self-will, and fear. It is critically important that these places are accepted, faced directly, acknowledged, and through our inner work, later transformed. If these areas are denied, suppressed, explained away, or otherwise avoided, then they do not have a chance to evolve. If they do not evolve, then they will continue to obscure the innermost part of us, the wise and empowered part that is connected to God. Thus the dark places that need to evolve are like the clouds obscuring the sun. The sun (the part in us connected with God) is always there, although it is often covered up.

If we can admit to having these unevolved aspects inside ourselves, and can acknowledge that they may make us occasionally vulnerable, needy, weak, irrational, wrong, fallible, and unhappy, then we can start the process of burning away these metaphorical clouds. In order to do this, we must let go of our defenses, the part that insists that everything be "right." In order to be able to let go of our defenses, we must start by acknowledging the truth that we humans, by our very nature, are not perfect. This can be a great relief, and the beginning of stepping into a new place where strength and independence, where fulfillment and insight, can all be brought forward in a way that is not otherwise possible. It is paradoxical, but in the admission of our imperfection, there lies the opportunity to move much more rapidly toward perfection.

To open to a connection with God, it is not necessary that a person be perfect. But to establish and expand this connection, to open to a greater wisdom, a greater power, a greater love, a greater truth, one must fight and work to overcome these dark aspects of the personality. To the extent that we emotionally insist on being perfect, on having others be perfect, and/or on having life be perfect, to that extent do we create unhappiness for ourselves and for others. Intellectually we may readily acknowledge that all these matters are characterized by imperfection; but our emotional experience nonetheless insists that only when these matters are perfect can we be happy. This is because the demand to have perfection is incompatible with reality, and this incompatibility cannot help but damage a human being's experience of happiness and joy.

Thus the imperfection of human beings itself is not something that we can change. It is a fact of life. We empower ourselves by instead focusing upon those matters that can be modified, those matters which are within the realm of our personal influence. Rebellion against that which is unchangeable is a waste of psychic energy. Discernment between matters that cannot be changed, and the matters which can, opens up a new perspective in which the practical steps to moving toward happiness and fulfillment can be perceived.

Personal Story:

Carla was very bright and impatient. She had a doctorate from a prestigious university and worked professionally as a psychologist. Because she had studied so much she felt as though she should have resolved her personal problems, because she was, after all, forty-five years old and had gone through a great deal of psychological training. She was also restless and judgmental about herself, especially because she was still single. As a coping mechanism, she would frequently slip into a perfect fantasy world where she would be in a marriage with an intelligent, successful, affluent, and good-looking man.

Her unfulfilled needs for intimacy, when combined with her great self-consciousness, made her needy and clingy. When she went out on dates with men, this needy and clingy attitude would often scare men away. She would typically approach men with what felt like an emotional tidal wave of demands. Although she knew that it was not advisable to articulate these demands on dates, nonetheless the men felt the emotional energy of her demands like "you must love me," and "you must fulfill my fantasy of what a perfect relationship should be like."

Her compulsive, impatient, pushy manner put men on the defensive, if they stayed around at all. Although she was, on another level, both a charming and loving woman, most of her relationships were very short-lived. This was because the men she dated felt as though they could never simply be themselves when they were with Carla.

After a long stretch of being without a lover, Carla looked more deeply at the patterns she was encountering with men. Several men who she had dated had revealed that they felt they would never be able to fulfill her expectations, never be enough, and never become the superman she wanted. She examined what she expected from a man, and came to appreciate that no man on this earth could deliver to her the perfect life that she thought she needed in order to be happy.

With a more realistic attitude, she was soon able to establish a romantic relationship with a local real estate agent. Although she and this man lived together for about a year, this man left Carla to go back to his ex-wife. Although this promising romantic relationship did end at that point, through this relationship Carla came to experientially understand that she could realistically have love in her life. She also learned that an important prerequisite to experiencing love was being clear about what she could realistically expect from men.

This relationship was furthermore important for Carla because she came to understand that her happiness increased markedly when she was willing to accept not only her own imperfection, but the imperfection of the man she was with. Her happiness increased the more objective she was about the fact that there was plenty of imperfection in her life. She also learned that she could not truly accept imperfection in her partner if she had not first accepted it in herself.

Journal Questions:

(1) In your life, what does perfection look like? Be specific and make a list of all the important attributes of the perfect life, as you see it. As you make this list, allow yourself to feel your resentment about not having some of these things in your life.

(2) Choose three of the most emotionally charged items on the list from the prior question. With respect to these three items, in what ways are your demands for perfection truly incompatible with what your life has to offer? For each of these three items, jot down a few ways in which your ideas of perfection are out of touch with reality. (Note that by doing this exercise, you are not shutting down the opportunity to manifest future possibilities; you are instead shutting down unnecessary sources of frustration.)

(3) In what ways would you personally need to grow, change, and expand your capacities, in order to manifest those aspects of your perfect life that are within the realm of the possible?

36

Navigating Expectations
Without a Forcing Current

Affirmation:

T HE CHILD WITHIN wants things handed to it on a silver plat-
ter, without first having paid the price in terms of decision-
making, self-responsibility, and work effort. As a mature adult,
I dialog with and reeducate my child within. I thereby arrive at
the place where I fully accept and engage with the prerequisites
to manifesting the life conditions that I seek.

Core Idea:

A forcing current is a subtle energetic pushing—a feeling that
something must be a certain way. Behind all forcing currents is
a demand of one type of another, whether articulated explicitly
or not, whether conscious or unconscious. The child in all of us,

no matter what our chronological age, knows only extremes. For example, it may demand that everybody love us, all the time, and express this love feeling in the ways we want them to express it. In child consciousness, only the great height of this achievement is accomplished, or else all is lost and nothing is accomplished.

In mature inner dialog with this child, we can examine its unreasonable demands, and its out-of-touch-with-the-world energetic forcing currents. We need to show the child within that the manifestation of the child's will is in many cases not a possibility in the real world. In the example just given, such a demand is clearly a fantasy. Some people will love us, and some will not. Even those special people who are emotionally close to us will love us only some of the time. And even those who clearly love us a great deal will sometimes express their love the way we want them to, and sometimes they won't. The mature adult in us realizes and accepts that experience in the world is always going to be a mixture of some things that we want, and some that we don't want.

In the realization that our unreasonable and out-of-touch childish demands will never be fulfilled, there can be a relaxing of the forcing current. Without the forcing current, a heavy burden will be removed from our metaphorical emotional shoulders. A hostility against both others and life will then be diminished—a hostility that was originally generated because our child within was unrealistically feeling deprived. In this place we will find much more fluidity and flexibility with both others and life.

For example, we can then allow other people the freedom to be whom they really are right now, the freedom to choose how they wish manifest in the world right now, and the freedom to inhabit whatever inner state they find themselves in right now. When we are in this place of acceptance and groundedness, our powers of observation will also be markedly enhanced. It is there that we will be more readily able to see, sense, and intuit what is true…not just what we wanted to be true. In this place, beyond the forcing current, is an open presence with life, a relaxed questioning about what is true.

The child within all of us also has a very limited sense of time. That child must have his way—right now—exactly the way he wants it, from everyone. The child within selfishly believes that only if his will is manifested immediately can he be happy. This may at first sound preposterous when expressed in such a blatant way, but as we take the time to honestly investigate its manifestation in our lives, we will discover just this type of outrageous one-sided childish demand inside us. We have covered it up with our mask, we have put a veneer of social acceptability around it, all with the hope that we won't be rejected or adversely judged. But when we go behind our mask, we will see that the anxiety, the tension, the pushing demand, and the struggle with life, all come exactly from this place.

The relinquishing of the forcing current, the allowing life to be exactly as it genuinely is, the accepting of everything just as it is now (including not having our way)—in that space we notice how the child within placed an exaggerated importance on having things turn out his way. We also notice how we became depressed, disappointed, angry, and emotionally reactive in response to not having our way, exactly as we wanted it. Here we will additionally notice that the child within has no sense of a past or a future, and no sense of the context in which we are making tangible progress working toward a big goal. In this more open space of relinquishing, we realize that the child within has no ability to evaluate the true significance of what is happening now, and what those things mean for our eventual fulfillment or lack thereof. It is with this realization that we can more readily take the child's demands down from the high place of importance, where we have placed those demands in the past.

When we look at the problems in our lives, and we honestly examine our emotional reactions to these problems, we will find both the demands and the forcing currents. The child within us believes it will be tragic if we do not obtain those things that we demand. But if we give up the demands that life conform to our expectations, if we let go of the forcing currents, then we will be free of a great inner tension. Paradoxically, then we will be free to receive something, although not necessarily what we previously sought. It may even be that what we receive will be more valuable than what we had previously desired. In this more expansive state, if we do not receive what we want, then not receiving it won't cause anywhere near the imagined level of distress that we believed it would.

Just calmly being in our present state, noticing and going with wherever we are in the moment, and having no judgment about whether our current situation is good or bad, brings a new and more empowered place to the changes that we want to make. Stepping back from the unrealistic demands and the forcing current gives us a detachment that could never have been achieved by superimposing "right" moralistic rules on top of the child consciousness. In this distance, in this breathing room, we can have a dialog with the child within, a dialog that objectively explores what is true, what is working, and what is not. In this stepping back, we will see the child consciousness is steeped in dualities, in a black or white world, in a struggle that feels like life or death. In this stepping back we will see the needless and counterproductive self-dramatization that our child within has brought to the condition where we do not get our way, exactly as we want it, right now.

Personal Story:

Miguel was in a statistics class with Rita, a woman whom he liked for several years and had gotten to know through college classes. The two of them would sometimes have lunch together, although they were not lovers. They talked on the phone and texted often, but they did not see each other at parties or go to the same social events, because he had a girlfriend, and she had a boyfriend. In the statistics class, they were both in a study group with a few other students who were also friends with both of them.

One day Miguel received a scathing email from Rita, an email copied to the whole study group. The email laid into him, criticizing his approach to the homework, his work ethic, and his competence to do college-level work. Miguel was dumbfounded, perplexed, and confused. He wondered why Rita would drag the others in the study group into this. He wondered what had gotten into her, because up to this point she had been so supportive, almost like a sister. He could think of nothing he had done to cause this attack. To make matters worse, in that email she had challenged him to answer her allegations via email, and to copy everyone else in the group with his response.

This situation provoked many feelings within Miguel. Over the last few years, he had come to rely on Rita as a trusted close friend, and these accusations seemed like a profound betrayal. He remembered how his mother would sometimes be quite critical of him, would yell and scream at him, and at other times be quite loving and supportive. That memory about his mother's fickle nature was distressing to dredge up again. He felt his child within coming forward to the present situation and demanding that all the women in his life be consistent. At this point, he wasn't sure if Rita was a friend or a foe. This not knowing who's side she was on was a very uncomfortable place for Miguel, and he noticed that he wanted to push Rita to take one side or the other.

On another level, Miguel felt as though there must be something else going on, because nothing about Rita's most recent communication seemed to make any sense to him. So rather than jumping into action, Miguel gave himself the luxury of a one-hour solo walk around the college campus. He took a pocket-sized paper notebook to write down a few ideas.

During the walk he realized he had a demand that Rita always support him, and that she always be on his side. Historically their relationship had in fact been something like that. To himself he admitted that this demand was unrealistic, and he then understood that he wanted her to be like the "good" (idealized) parent that he never experienced. He consciously chose to let go of that demand, and with this thought at the same time he felt a relaxing and release of tension in his shoulders. Up until that point, he had not paid attention to how much of the tension surrounding this situation he was holding in his shoulders.

During the walk, he also felt a social expectation to defend himself, notably to maintain his honor in front of the study group, but at the same time he felt this traditional approach to the dispute was most likely ill advised. Instead, at least initially, he chose to devote himself to hearing Rita out, and understanding where she was coming from. He also chose not to involve the study group, and called her up on his cell phone instead. He opened the conversation with a receptive and flexible question, simply asking: "What's going on?"

Rita stridently then repeated her complaints about how he was acting, how he was being, and how he was treating her. It was on this last point that he picked up a thread of the cause that had led to her accusations. Rita had recently broken up with her boyfriend, and she had let Miguel know that she was interested in having an intimate relationship with him. But Miguel was already in a committed monogamous relationship, and he had already told Rita that. Nonetheless, Rita had recently repeatedly upped the ante in the "let's get together" game, by getting more and more suggestive with Miguel. She even made a statement about her availability, and how he shouldn't miss this opportunity, in front of the whole study group.

In spite of Miguel's fear that he was going to lose the relationship with Rita because he was honest with her, on the phone he reiterated his position, which was that he was already in a committed monogamous relationship, and that he was not leaving that relationship. He then admitted his fear that he would lose his friendship with Rita because he didn't give her what she wanted. The floodgates then opened, and Rita's feelings came pouring out. It turned out that she was upset that her feelings for Miguel were not reciprocated, and that Miguel had taken no action in response to her attempts at becoming more romantically involved. Rita admitted that in her accusations, she felt a bit of revenge. She explained that she was also still upset about her recent breakup with her boyfriend, and she didn't feel that Miguel was supporting her with that either.

In a courageous space of just accepting things with Rita exactly as they were—seemingly terribly screwed-up and damaged forever—Miguel brought the conversation back to her email accusations, going over them calmly one by one. Through this calm and focused discussion, Miguel saw that her attacks were basically an indication that she didn't feel supported by him, and didn't feel as though he was listening to her. In this open and receptive place, Rita experienced how Miguel showed up the way she wanted him to (although not romantically). She admitted that the topics mentioned in the email were just provocations, not substantive points. After Miguel understood how Rita was feeling, he could let go of the content of the email, of his need to defend himself, and of his need to maintain his honor. A very healing and intimate conversation, lasting about an hour, then took place. At the end of this more intimate conversation, Rita agreed to send an email apology to Miguel, which was to be copied to all the study group members.

These days, now that they both have graduated from college, even though they live in distant cities, Miguel and Rita still maintain contact every month or so via Skype and the phone. Miguel is married, but Rita is still looking for Mr. Right. But whatever their marital situation, Miguel and Rita have resolved to be supportive soul friends for each other.

Journal Questions:

(1) What form do your daydreams take when it comes to resolving the serious problem that vexes you, the matter that you so ardently wish to change? Rather than imposing the fixed solutions that you have in daydreams,

what would happen if you were to flexibly embrace what is now true? Would there be more inner mobility in this space—mobility that might better support you to pursue a viable real-world solution?

(2) Consider that your demands involving the situation you wish to change are the result of your inner child's self-centeredness. Can you let down your insistence to have your way right now? Can you instead expand your vision, so that the needs of everyone involved can be embraced? Residing in this more holistic viewpoint for a moment, would it not be more mature to embrace what is right for everyone involved? How might you personally need to change as a result of living with this more mature viewpoint?

(3) If there are other people associated with your serious problem, people with whom you have some issues, can you imagine granting them the freedom to be the way they choose? What would that look like? Could you give them genuine respect, no matter whether or not they met your demands? Now, can you give yourself that same freedom to be yourself, and also give yourself genuine respect, whether or not life has met your demands?

37

Discovering and Transcending Your Negative Intentionality

Affirmation:

I ASK FOR divine guidance so that I may clearly see the part in me that senselessly, wastefully, destructively, and irrationally refuses to change. I ask that I may be shown all resistances that block me from admitting the existence of this negative intentionality. I resolve to plow through all those resistances, so that I may then come to a place of positively creating my life.

Core Idea:

For many people, it is not enough to have revealed their fears, their selfish willfulness, and their unjustifiable pride. It is not enough for them to see how these and other lower-self aspects, the unevolved parts of their personality, have been keeping them stuck. There is another important factor that must be addressed, and that topic is discussed in this chapter.

But before you the reader can benefit from this chapter, you must have already plumbed the depths of your psyche, and you must have honestly identified and admitted all the conscious reasons why you would like to continue to maintain the status quo, why you do not want to change. Similarly, to benefit most from this chapter, you must also have prayed for divine assistance that you might give over to, and thereafter genuinely support, a new and positive approach to life. If you have not already done these things, your time is best spent working with the earlier chapters of this book, and then later coming back to this chapter.

Consider that humans unconsciously want those things that they fear. Also consider that we humans unconsciously desire those things that we experience, even if these were negative experiences. Both of these assertions are quite empowering—if we allow them to be. Both affirm that we are creating our experience on earth, and that we do not need to be a victim of another person, a set of circumstances, or any other external influence. This is not to say that others don't do cruel, hurtful or thoughtless things, or that in life we don't face a set of challenging circumstances. Without question, external influences exist and they decidedly do affect us. But for all of us, we are the central, the first and foremost, and the most important cause creating our experience of life.

So even though we make good progress with all our personal inner work, we may still feel stuck, may still feel unable to proceed with a change, and/or may feel unable to sustain the change we consciously seek to make. Why is that? What is holding us back? We will call this influence "negative intentionality." Here we are talking about a fundamental "no" to life, a fundamental refusal to change. Negative intentionality is not rational, and it does not respond to rational inner or outer dialogs. Negative intentionality does not want to give, to contribute, to love, to move out into the world, to receive, and/or to assist us in living a fruitful life. At first this notion that we have such a thing inside each of us may sound unbelievable. But to benefit from this important information, and the suggested personal process that goes along with it, it is essential that we remain open to this concept.

This negative intentionality wants to hate, wants to be spiteful, and wants to withhold itself. It doesn't matter what good reasons to change you throw at it, the answer is always a resounding: "NO!" It doesn't matter what the consequences are, negative intentionality just wants its way, which is a senseless destructiveness. While this apparently unreachable part of us may sound intimidating, it is possible to change it with the aid of divine assistance. This part of us is in error, and it needs to be reeducated. We should keep in mind that here we are talking about a small but nonetheless influential part of our lower self.

Note that we are not talking about who we are at a fundamental level, which is ultimately (after we have transformed this part) our higher self. Part of our job in life is to identify, get to know, engage with, and evolve our lower self—including the evolution of this negative intentionality. The fact that we can see the negative intentionality, can feel it, can watch it in our life, all that collectively means that there is another different part of us which is the observer (our higher self). Thus, although this negative intentionality is a part of each of us, it is not a permanent part. Like the rest of the lower self, it is temporary, and it will later become part of the higher self when it matures and evolves.

To the extent that this negative intentionality remains in our unconscious, to the extent that it continues to hide in the darkness of the lower self, it will have great power over us. If we can recognize it, and come to understand how it operates, how it, for example, blocks the change we wish to make, it will be disempowered. This is because we can call this part of us on its games, we can show it how its strategy creates nothing of true value, and we can refuse to pursue the course of action that it advocates. Self-discipline is a very important part of spiritual practice in general, especially when it comes to transforming negative intentionality.

To get to this place of mastering our negative intentionality, first we must overcome our resistance to acknowledging the fact that such a thing exists inside us. This is a time for humility and acceptance, a time for each of us to be willing to look less than perfect. To bring our negative intentionality into focus, we must notice that some of our actions are destructive and senseless. We need to see in what areas we feel unable or unwilling to change, or how we steadfastly refuse to change, even in the face of overwhelmingly positive benefits to ourselves associated with that same change. We need to notice how we act in an inexplicably damaging manner, in ways that cause ourselves deprivation and suffering, but we don't know why. It is in these inner places that our negative intentionality is likely to be at work.

The shift that must come about is for us to clearly see that it is each one of us, and not any outside force, that wants to create senseless wasteful destruction. We are the ones who intend to be negative, intend to remain deprived, intend to keep suffering, and intend stay in isolation. This part of us feels hate, spite, the desire to inflict punishment, and other negative emotions. We must see that each of us wants to hold onto a way of operating that is fundamentally negative.

So the way to liberate ourselves from our negative intentionality is to acknowledge that this way of behaving, this way of interacting with life is coming from inside each one of us. Negative intentionality is sourced out of a part of us that wants to be this way. This is why we use the word "intentionality" when referring to this part of us. When we understand that it comes from inside us, then we have a choice. Our life shows up as a result of the cumulative choices that we each have made up to this point in time. Having a new choice opens a new door, opens the possibility of being a different way. Identifying ourselves primarily as our higher self, knowing that we are significantly more than this negative intentionality, that stance will facilitate our efforts to make the choice to be another way (more mature, more loving, more compassionate, more heart-felt, etc.).

To see and come to terms with our negative intentionality is a major step in our personal spiritual evolution. Achieving this goal will require struggle, effort, and patience. There is a part within each of us that denies the existence of this negative intentionality. We must first pay attention to this part. This is a key step that cannot be skipped over.

But this spiritual development process is not just about vaguely identifying this negative intentionality. We must deeply understand our fundamental stubbornness, our unwillingness to move and change. To accomplish this, our ego (our conscious, willing, and acting mind) must team-up with our higher self (our God-connected part), so that we may then successfully grapple with our negative intentionality. This alliance between the ego and the higher self will in turn allow each of us to choose to adopt a positive attitude, in which we genuinely want to be positive, want to make a contribution, want to give our best, and of course, want to change.

Every moment, through our conscious choices, we vote which side of us will get our conscious attention. We can vote to side with our negative intentionality and lower self, and thereby for continuing to be in a stuck and painful place. Or we can vote to side with the alliance between the ego and the higher self, and thereby for living a constructive and positive life. Vote now and consistently thereafter for the latter ticket of candidates; vote for making and sustaining the big change that has so dominated your consciousness recently. Vote now, and again, and again, etc., for the alliance of the ego with the higher self, so that your improved self-government can then go on to create the life that you yearn for.

Personal Story:

Alicia came from a poor immigrant family with severe financial problems and a very difficult uncertain legal status. As a result she always felt deprived, and always felt as though some financial disaster lurked just around the corner. She was also badly beaten by her mother and severely criticized by her father.

As a young adult in her twenties, she had virtually no self-esteem. This lack of self-esteem caused her to abort and turn away from a number of opportunities that might have turned out positively for her. For example, she dropped out of high school, and didn't seem to be able to complete any particular job-training program, even though she had tried to go through a number of them. She wasn't in any way deficient mentally, so intelligence was not the issue.

Although she went from one clerical office job to another, never staying anywhere more than a year, what really bothered her most was the way she kept walking away and turning away from intimate relationships with men. She really wanted to have an intimate partner, a lover, a man with whom she could share her life. Many men were interested in her, so attractiveness was not the issue either. In every case, whenever her relationships with a new man seemed to be working out, when the prospect of being happy in her love life loomed on the horizon, then she would sabotage things and promptly exit from the relationship.

This process seemed to be an immediate response to the moment when the man deeply decided he wanted to be with Alicia, when he gave himself over to the relationship. As soon as Alicia noticed this, she would start a fight, or create a dramatic and acrimonious scene, or in some other way generate a justification for exiting the relationship. Sometimes these men would pursue her, although most of the time her blowout was outrageous and serious enough so that the men would stay away. Even when a select few still pursued her, her cruelty and mean words caused these remaining men to soon leave. Later she would again feel lonely, and wallow in her low opinion of herself.

After this whole process with men had repeated itself eight painful times, enough for Alicia to realize that some twisted pattern was involved, she sought some professional assistance. A therapist worked with her on why she would sabotage and exit just when things were looking good with these men. There were the usual explanations like her fear of being dominated and controlled, abused and beaten, in effect repeating the relationship she had with her mother. But during the therapy process, she got into another relationship with an eligible man, and again she sabotaged and exited at the predictable point in time. The fact that she repeated the destructive process again, even though she was in therapy, was enough to cause Alicia to leave the therapist, claiming that therapy didn't work.

Soon after that, she began a deeper process with a priest named Jesse. He brought up the notion of negative intentionality, the concept of a part in her that didn't want to change, that wanted to continue the senseless, destructive, wasteful process of aborting relationships with men that seemed promising. Because she was in so much pain about the whole process, she did not have much resistance to this unusual concept. Upon further discussion with him, she came to appreciate that there was in fact a part of her that enjoyed this lower-self process, a part that believed that if she let go of it, she would then be forced to let go of this little bit of pleasure that her largely depressing and deprived lifestyle afforded her.

The next meeting with Jesse revealed that the sabotage and exit process was Alicia's way of expressing her hatred and anger at her parents. At the child level, coming from her negative intentionality, she felt that if her life were a mess, particularly her love life, then she would show her parents what a horrible job they had done with her. Coming from this negative intentionality, she figured that if she felt unhappy and was decidedly not manifesting the life she wanted, then she might cause her parents grief and distress. Alicia was surprised to see how much pleasure she got from the spite and revenge involving her parents (who were then still alive).

Through further discussions with Jesse, she discovered that the negative intentionality was really only hurting her, not her parents. So even if she chose to continue to attempt to cause them grief and distress, her negative intentionality strategy wasn't working. With Jesse she was later able to reach a place of both desiring to make a new and different choice with men, and also desiring and asking for divine assistance to make this positive change.

After taking this personal work a bit further, Alicia was later able to stay in relationships with men, although she would still from time to time feel the part in her that would impulsively want to sabotage and exit. At the time of this writing she had been in a loving relationship with a man for two years, a record length of time for her.

Journal Questions:

(1) In what ways have you been creating false hope for yourself when it comes to the big change that you seek to make? In what ways have you been creating impossible solutions, solutions that, deep down inside of you, you know have no

chance of working? Have you been creating and playing with these false hope solutions because fundamentally you do not want to change? Has this negative intentionality ruled your life, a search for a smoke screen, something that you can point to and then say: "But I have tried this and that, and nothing seems to work"?

(2) Once you have identified your own version of negative intentionality, and how it manifests in your life, ask yourself: "Why exactly am I holding onto it?" Are you unwilling to assume self-responsibility? Are you punishing your parents? Does the child in you feel as though she will lose her identity if she were to stop saying "no"? Don't just go with one of these possible explanations, but discover your own unique reasons for holding onto this negative intentionality.

(3) When it comes to letting go of your negative intentionality, what part of you is still saying: "I can't do this..."? Make a list of all the specific reasons why you can't make the shift to a place where you trust and believe in yourself, where you take a chance that it might be possible to complete the change that you so ardently seek. After you have written up your list, go back over it, and then ask yourself whether it is not really an issue of "I won't" rather than "I can't." If it is truly a matter of "I won't," then you have a choice. If you can see it is a matter of "I won't," then contemplate what it would mean to you to make a choice here.

38

Initiating a Grounded
Leap into the Unknown

Affirmation:

Today I consider the possibility that there is nothing to fear about the change I seek. Today I take one realistic, grounded, and constructive step forward, even though I may still have some fear. With this movement, I use a grounded faith, based on my demonstrated ability to expand, learn, and accommodate new ways of being.

Core Idea:

The day-to-day condition of humans is largely that of duality, in which we see things in terms of opposing extremes. Here we perceive life situations in black or white, good or bad, life or death, and day or night. Duality distorts reality. This is true when it comes to faith as well as many other areas.

Among intellectuals and the highly educated, faith often has a bad name. It is perceived as ungrounded belief, a blind trusting without evidence, a gullible wishful thinking borne out of laziness and ignorance. From this vantage point, faith understandably has a bad reputation. With this view, a rational person would want to guard himself against anything that might even remotely resemble faith. But consider a new possibility, which holds that this viewpoint is simply one end of a dualistic spectrum.

At the other end of this dualistic spectrum, we may feel as though we will always be blind to what is really going on in life. Here we believe we will always be groping in the dark, and seemingly floating in a groundless place. In this place we may believe in magic and deny our own responsibility for what's happening in our lives. In this alternate position on the spectrum, we rationalize that we don't have to do the hard work necessary to bring about the change we desire. Here, everything will come to us if we only believe the right thoughts. In this place, we don't have to grapple with the painful reality of the current situation, because it will all turn out, if only we really deeply believe, thinking that it will enough to turn the matter over to God or our higher self.

When we go beyond this duality, we can come to a deeper and more practical understanding of genuine faith. We can then discover that a grounded and realistic faith is actually an important ingredient in our personal transformational processes. It is with this non-dualistic understanding of faith that we can go on to successfully bring about the difficult change that we so ardently desire.

In this alternative grounded type of faith, we embrace all the unpleasant and unpalatable aspects of our current situation. Here we embrace the difficulties, the disorder, the looking bad, the feelings that come up, and all the other seemingly horrible and undesirable aspects of our current situation. In this place we are in truth, and when we align with truth, we align with the universe and with God. We can become self-responsible, and see ourselves as major contributors to the situation. In this respect, we embrace the fact that we are manifestations of God, that we too have creative power. In the embracing of our creative power, we see that we have the ability to create something else besides our current situation, notably we have the power to bring about the change we desire.

Of course, making a big change will always involve going through some fear and anxiety. We don't know what it will be like after we make the change. This not knowing seems scary and undesirable. In this place, as long as we don't make the big change, the fear of and anxiety about the unknown will continue to block us from proceeding. But what if, instead of dualistically considering change as an all-or-nothing situation, we could gradually build-up a genuine faith, a grounded and realistic faith? What if we successfully took a series of positive and constructive steps in the direction of making the desired change? Then our faith would be based on reality, not some magical story. We would then be taking self-responsibility, not expecting others to make the change for us. We would then be willing to fully pay the price necessary to bring about the change, and in that respect we would be in reality.

So many of us view the process of change like a circus trapeze act, where we let go of one swing high in the air, so that we can then take a grip on another swing. Emotionally we fear that we won't properly grasp the new swing, that our hands will slip, and that we will fall from a great height. Rather than upsetting ourselves with scary images such as this, what if we viewed the change process as something we have already been through many times? Rather than puffing it up with big-time drama, what if we regarded the change process as a normal part of life, something that we all must go through? What if we emotionally approached change as though we were on safe and firm ground? What if, as we saw it, there was really no big risk of falling from those great heights? What if we could now choose to take a series of small, manageable, and constructive steps? Wouldn't the process of change then become so much more inviting?

So the real concept of faith, the true concept of faith, goes beyond duality. When in this space, we must first contemplate a new way of operating, consider a new way of being, and imagine that things could be different. To begin this process, we must seriously be open to a new possibility. Here we must clearly see the undesirable aspects associated with remaining in our current situation. For example, we must feel our guilt for the harm that we have caused others, because we did not change. Here we must also feel the pain of the destructive repetition of our stubborn refusal to make the change that, on a deeper level, we know we must make. Here we must additionally understand the missed opportunities that have gone by us because we held onto our resistance about making this change.

To make room for this new possibility to manifest, to create the circumstances conducive to proceeding with the change we seek, we must employ this correct understanding of faith. Here we admit that there are things about which we currently know nothing. We do not, for example, know what it will be like to be on the other side of the change we seek. This is the first step in the direction of knowing a genuine faith. Here we admit that there is something beyond that which we can currently see. In this admission we are not being unrealistic, gullible, or unintelligent. In fact, the contrary is true. Those who do not admit that there is anything beyond that which they see, touch, and immediately experience indeed have narrow and limited minds.

Without a willingness to take a leap into the unknown, there can be no expansion, no change, and no growth for us. In order to change within ourselves, we must make room for alternatives not yet experienced. Rather than being ungrounded, this openness is actually fully consistent with the scientific way of looking at life. With this attitude, we consider new alternatives. Here we adopt an inquiring, open, humble, objective, and honest approach. With this attitude we experiment, and pay close attention to what works and what does not. And through our progress, through our diligent constructive steps forward, we build a genuine faith. With this expanded faith we come increasingly to believe that we can and will accomplish the big change that we have set out to accomplish.

Personal Story:

Peter was a healthy middle-aged man who had been working in a blue-collar factory job for many years. Through a serious but not-life-threatening industrial accident he became unexpectedly disabled. Although he received insurance payments to cover his living and medical expenses, and the prognosis for a full recovery was good, the accident came as a great shock to him. His life had been predictable and stable up until the time of the accident. Then everything all of a sudden seemingly fell apart.

All his life Peter had a great love of the law, the legal process, and the social importance of the political process. He had, for example, watched just about every movie he could find that dealt with lawyers. For many years he had been dreaming of being a lawyer. Although he had a bachelor's degree in political science, and could therefore enter law school directly, attending law school had remained for him a far away and unachievable goal.

Besides, given his modest financial situation and relatively low-paying job, Peter wondered how he could possibly get the money to go to law school. As the years went by, the prospect of going to law school seemed an unrealistic fantasy, something that he should get over, so that he could get on with the rest of his life. And then there was the prospect of all the demanding studying that three years of law school required. Peter had many doubts as well as little faith about his ability to meet these demands.

He decided to use his period of rehabilitation as a time of personal growth and an investigation into the many roadblocks he'd built related to preparing for law school. He proceeded in a light and inquiring way, as if law school was a game. He asked himself: "Why not at least investigate the possibilities?" By taking one constructive step after another, he built-up faith in his capacity to actually go through law school.

One of the roadblocks involved his capacity to do the challenging, intellectual work. It had been decades since he was in college, and he sincerely doubted that he could get through law school without flunking out. He challenged this thought, and read a few books about what it was like to go through law school. He asked a number of lawyers whether they thought he had a chance of success. To his surprise, the more that he investigated the question of law school, the more feasible it appeared to be.

He discovered that his temperament and personality traits, such as an eye for detail, matched those of successful lawyers. Through standardized tests, he learned that his intelligence level was above normal, and was therefore sufficient to be successful in law school. His confidence in himself and in his ability to make it through law school was growing.

Now that Peter's injury was healing, and he was able to return to his current factory work, his employer wanted him to return to work full-time. Peter worried that he wouldn't have the time to attend law school if he was employed full-time. He also didn't have the resources to take three years off from work so as to devote himself exclusively to law school. Since he was neither a woman nor a minority, the chances of a scholarship appeared to be low to nonexistent. This seemed to be the end of the story about his attending law school.

But he persistently researched law schools and found a new one that he could attend over the Internet. By attending part-time, law school would take him four years. On-line school also eliminated the need to commute, and he could continue his employment, so the resources question was handled. The possibility of going to law school was starting to look more like a realistic possibility, and Peter was getting excited about the prospect of actually manifesting his goal.

He next started worrying about his age. He was, after all, in his late fifties, and "What business," he thought, "... does a man at that advanced age have going to law school?" Peter spent time investigating whether older people were actually able to handle such challenging intellectual work. He was pleased to read recent brain research studies showing that the brain was plastic in nature, and so in reality was more able to adapt to new circumstances than most people currently believed.

While doing this research, he also connected with his deep desire to make a lasting contribution to society by generating a wider conversation about ethics, laws, and the ways that people interact with not only each other, but also with the environment. Connecting with his calling, and his desire to fulfill this calling by being a lawyer, he explored a new inner place of being willing to do whatever it took to getting through law school, passing the bar exam, and becoming licensed to practice law.

It was through these small but positive steps that Peter moved toward his dream. Last we heard, he had been admitted to, and received a partial scholarship from, the on-line law school of his choice. Halfway through his first semester, he felt expanded and challenged. He also felt blessed, and was relaxing into an allowing place where his life opened-up in a constructive and positive way. For Peter, he experienced an inner expansion and acceptance that he could find all he needed to manifest his dreams, all he needed in order to bring about the big change that he so desired.

Journal Questions:

(1) Consider that perhaps you are, like all of us, a manifestation of divine reality. If that possibility exists, it stands to reason that divine creative power exists within you. Given your current difficulties, however, that

power probably manifests at the moment in a diminished form. As an experiment, ask that place within yourself to show you a new possibility, a new way of functioning, a new way of approaching the change that you want to make. Tell it that you will genuinely be receptive to receiving an answer, whether that answer will come immediately or sometime in the near future. Affirm that you are flexible and open here, that you will continue to be receptive to getting an answer in whatever form it may take.

(2) Think back and remember a time when you tried something new, something big that you had not previously considered yourself capable of achieving. Remember how you let go of your rigid holding on, and how you stopped stubbornly refusing to change. Remember when and how you were willing to entertain a new possibility. How were you then? In a grounded faith, in a knowing that you can—and in fact have already—moved ahead constructively, could you bring that same place to the change that you now wish to make?

(3) In terms of the change you wish to make, recognize that strong fear exists within you. This fear believes that when something happens contrary to your will, the result will be dangerous. Now, adopting the strategy of a scientist, objectively investigate this fear. Specifically what about not getting your way would be so dangerous? Make a list of all the dangerous aspects, and then methodically compare them to reality. One by one, ask: "Is this really

true?" Then, examining each aspect on its own, determine whether you have blown the level of danger out of proportion. To the extent that you have shown this place of fear that a change is not really as dangerous as it believed, to that extent you have taken a constructive step forward. Now, what would your next constructive step forward look like? Imagine that.

39

Risking the Disapproval
of Others

Affirmation:

I RELINQUISH THE dependent need for the constant approval, affection, and admiration of others. I instead open to my own deeper truth as the pathway to discover my own right course of action.

Core Idea:

Many of us are compelled to do things because we feel as though it's a matter of "emotional survival." For example, we may feel that we absolutely must have the approval of another person. Perhaps this person is a parent, a spouse, an employer, or someone else with great influence and/or authority in our lives. The more we cater to and try to please this person, the less we think of ourselves.

In reality, true emotional survival is strictly dependent on our self-concept, not on the opinions of others. Many of us walk around with a misconception that we require others to approve of us, not just at a specific time, but all of the time. This is a very high standard, and that standard is likely to be nearly impossible to meet. Our lives can become still more dysfunctional if we don't really understand what others want of us, but instead operate based on our history or what we think others want from us.

To free ourselves up, this bondage to the opinion of others must be rigorously challenged, no matter how subtle its manifestation in our lives may be. Many of us conceal this dependency in artful and deceptive ways, but it still exists. This bondage may take the form of being unwilling to leave a job that we hate, for example, because we believe that our identity is intimately tied-up with our job. We think that if we did not have this important job, then people would not approve of us or hold us with great respect.

All of us unconsciously believe that if we receive the attention, admiration, and approval of others, then we feel as though our worth in the world has been established. On the other hand, if we can't receive these things, then we believe we have just been shown to be inferior. Thus each of us, on some emotional level, is claiming self-importance, and calling out for others to validate our self-importance. According to one's temperament, this claim for self-importance may be quite easy for others to detect, or it might be subtle and concealed.

If you follow this tendency deeply into your soul, you will find a part of you that wants to be special and unique. This part erroneously believes that if you are extra special in the eyes of the world, it will compensate for your feelings of inferiority. This part believes this special status will overshadow and overcome these feelings of inferiority. But no amount of approval, affection, and attention from others can compensate for a lack of belief and trust in yourself.

Nor does the answer lie in rebelling against the perceived need for admiration, affection, and approval. For example, we will find no answer if we are demonstrating our independence from these sought-after experiences. Instead the answer lies in having the courage to look at the truth, in having the courage to see how we have put ourselves in chains, in how we have kept ourselves back with unnecessary limits and self-defeating concepts. The answer involves going beyond the questions "what would others expect?" and "what am I supposed to do?" By getting in touch with ourselves, we can overcome the compulsion to seek the approval of others, as well as the compulsion to reject this approval of others. It is then that we can find the right middle way, which is the unifying truth for which our soul calls out.

True self-confidence, a true high self-regard, comes from being honest with oneself, and doing one's personal work. It stems from having the courage to face what's happening in this moment, and the courage to take responsibility for one's part in creating these circumstances. It comes from being willing to change in light of the information that has been learned, and being willing to grow and evolve as life demands that of us. True self-confidence issues from the willingness to independently examine the issues, to make up our own mind, to go beyond "the rules" that other people tell us. True self-confidence does not come from compliance with the rules and regulations, nor does it come from conformity with the desires of others, but from the courage to be our own person, to stand in our own truth, and to act accordingly. True self-confidence comes from the willingness to make a mistake, and the courage to try something new, not from the fact that a mistake was or was not made.

Personal Story:

Elaine was having an affair with a married man. One day she discovered that she was pregnant. She wanted to keep the baby, but she knew that her traditional family would not approve because she was not married to the father. Since she lived in a city far away from her family, she had infrequent contact with them. During the early months of her pregnancy, she spent a great deal of time fretting about her mother's reaction, and the reaction of her mother's new husband, who was both an arch-conservative and staunchly religious.

Pressed for details of the pregnancy during a phone conversation with Elaine's mother, one of Elaine's sisters made up a story about Elaine getting pregnant with sperm from a sperm bank. Elaine didn't know what to tell her mother about her affair, so she went along with this ruse. This deception went on for many months, and all the while Elaine kept feeling more and more guilty about not telling her mother the truth. Shortly thereafter Elaine's mother passed away because she had been battling with cancer for many years.

Elaine's mother never got to meet the father of Elaine's son. She would probably have been delighted to know that her grandson had a real flesh-and-blood father. In subsequent years, the father went on to divorce his-then wife, and move in with Elaine and their son. The father of her son got to know Elaine's family, and the three of them had many years of joyous time together before this man also died of cancer.

Many years later, looking back on her experience with her mother, Elaine regretted not telling her mother the truth about her pregnancy early on, regretted how her lies spun out of control and had to be embellished in order to look consistent. She also regretted how these lies had needlessly distanced her from her mother, precisely at a time when she could have greatly benefitted from her mother's advice and support.

That time of her life, when she was pregnant with a child and the father was married to another woman, was a very lonely time for Elaine. Her own shame caused her to hide and cover-up her situation, caused her to be much more isolated than she would have liked to have been in retrospect. She wasn't quite sure how to talk about her situation with people, and so avoided talking about it at all, except with a few very close friends. Ironically her concern about acceptance caused her loneliness and isolation at a time universally understood to be when women need more support.

Elaine furthermore regretted how she had been so insistent on her mother's constant approval, and how she could not bear the thought of losing her mother's love. In retrospect, Elaine saw the situation as a big missed opportunity with her mother. With the perspective she has today, Elaine would have done things very differently. She would, for example, have been much more forthright, and would then have been able to be more comfortable with the simple truth of what was actually happening.

Elaine also realized that she had made an erroneous assumption about how her mother would react to the news. In retrospect, Elaine recognized that her mother most likely would not have reacted the way that Elaine had feared. Because she was all tied-up by her fears about being rejected at the time when she was pregnant, Elaine had underestimated her mother's capacity for compassion. After all, Elaine's mother was a nurse, and she showed compassion to her patients frequently. In addition, Elaine's mother had been wrestling with her own cancer for years, and had recently nursed Elaine's father on his death bed as he died from emphysema. Life had expanded Elaine's mother's capacity for compassion in many ways. But at the time of her pregnancy, somehow, strangely, Elaine didn't believe that her mother would have been compassionate with her.

Journal Questions:

(1) In what areas do you believe you must have the approval of others? Specifically, what opinion(s) must other people have of you?

(2) For what perceived inferiority do you believe the approval of others will compensate? Is this belief in fact grounded— in other words, is it true that you are inferior? Could it be that you are just different from others in this respect?

(3) Consider your interaction with others in the area where you are currently having trouble, in the area where you wish to change. If you were to let go of the need for others' approval, what would you do? What would that look like? Stretch yourself into seriously considering that possibility.

40

Using Your Will Most Productively

Affirmation:

I COMMIT TO keep honestly and objectively checking-in with myself. I repeatedly ask for divine guidance, so that I may be able to deeply understand my inner currents, feelings, emotions, conflicts, and misconceptions. I pray that I may come to understand how these inner states cause me to create certain experiences out in the world.

Core Idea:

Our lives will change markedly when we discover certain truths. These truths will give our lives a new direction, a new purpose, and a deeper meaning. There are places in our psyche where we are tied-up, and these places of bondage block us from seeing our own personal important truths. If we untie these knots in our psyches, if we unravel these knots that keep us bound-up inside, then we can move with life, then we can make the changes that we want to make.

These truths, the truths that will change our lives, do not come to us gratuitously—we have to earn them. We must go through the process of searching for these truths, and we must grope in the dark for clues that will lead us to these truths. And once we discover these truths, we must ponder their meaning, and how we might use them to change our lives. We must be committed to the multi-step process of self-discovery in order to most powerfully accelerate our own personal development. With God's help, we feed ourselves spiritual truth thereby.

A similar multi-step process exists for the physical food that we eat. In the latter case, if we live in an industrialized economy, generally we must earn money for food, we must buy the food from a store, we must prepare it, we must serve it, and we must eat it. We should not expect that learning the most important truths of our lives would be any different. Thus the process of getting spiritual nourishment is similar to the process of getting physical nourishment in that multiple steps are involved.

Searching for these truths, a process that might be called finding "spiritual nourishment," can take many forms. It can be achieved by an intimate discussion with a friend, by meditation or prayer, by taking a walk alone in the woods, by writing in one's journal, or by reading enlightened words. But in order to accelerate the process of finding spiritual nourishment, one must wage an inner battle. In order to move ahead with this self-discovery process, one must fight and triumph over the inner voice that says things that block the process like: "I am too tired today," or "what difference does it make if I skip a day," or "I'm not in the mood right now."

We will certainly have other opportunities, if we do not chose to do this self-discovery work today. But if we give in to our lower selves here, if we take the path of least resistance, we will be starving our souls. Inwardly we yearn to expand, to evolve, to grow, and to mature. It is the unevolved, lazy, childish part in each of us that wants things to be done for us, that does not want to step up to full adult responsibility. This lazy part that does not want to change will discourage us from doing the self-discovery work, because we might then go on to make the big change that we consciously desire. We must identify this lazy part, and discover how it causes us to defeat our conscious desires. We must monitor our inner reactions, inner feeling currents, and our inner states, and look for everything that would block us from, and everything that would get in the way of, making the change that we desire.

We cleanse our bodies regularly, and we have no argument with the fact that washing and bathing is a necessity if we are going to keep our body healthy. Yet we often object to doing the same thing with our psyche. We think it is asking too much to regularly (hopefully daily) examine what goes on inside of us, to challenge certain unevolved aspects of our inner states, to pray for assistance in the transformation of those aspects, and to deliberately set out to evolve those aspects. In this respect, maintaining spiritual hygiene is not too far different from the process of maintaining physical hygiene, in that regularity and diligence make a big difference.

One of the most productive uses of our will is to establish and maintain positive and constructive habits. To regularly cleanse our souls, to regularly engage in self-reflection and self-discovery will help us a great deal in our efforts to change. Through this process we can actually change our feelings and emotions. Although feelings and emotions cannot be changed instantly or on command, they can change gradually and organically, over time, as a by-product of changing our thinking. This is because our feelings and emotions are generated by our thinking. If we no longer have a troublesome thought, then we will no longer initiate the troublesome feelings and emotions that come with that thought. Without these troublesome feelings and emotions, we will be much more likely to be able to make the change, and maintain the change that we wish to make.

To turbo-charge our personal change process, we must enlist our willpower, and we must bring it to bear on the process of our own personal development. We must know that the speed of productive change in our lives will be notably slowed, and perhaps stopped altogether, if we do not focus on our own self-discovery. On the other hand, our complaints and objections about the life we now experience are a good mirror, showing us how we keep deferring this process, how we keep turning away from the process of self-discovery.

We must know that if we change our consciousness, we will then naturally change our personal experience. If we change our personal experience, we will change our behavior. And if we change our personal experience, we will also change our relationships. We can then not only change what's possible for us in the world, but we also open up a new pathway to manifesting the change that we consciously desire.

For example, if we sincerely examine what's going on within us, often we will discover that we still have the same reactions we had to a long-past situation, or perhaps to a long-past ongoing condition. The current situation we encounter may be entirely different, but we still hold onto, and still express, the same old reactions. These reactions are obsolete, and they can be destructive to our current situation in life. Unless we are willing to examine and challenge these left over reactions, willing to search for their origins and clearly see that they are not creating the results we want, we will not be able to change them. And the way to do that search is to have a diligent, regular, habitual, and dedicated spiritual practice, as described above.

Personal Story:

Cecilia was distraught because she believed it was important for a woman to be married, and she had been searching for a long time for the right guy to marry. She was forty-five years old, but had never found the right man. As she told a friend of hers, every guy she went out on dates with was too controlling, and was hell-bent on running her life. She was angry at men in general because they consistently seemed intent on telling her what to do. Cecilia told many other people about her opinion of dating, saying essentially the same thing over and over.

Tired of hearing the same old story, one of Cecilia's close friends gently broached that same topic with her, saying that the one common denominator in all these relationships was Cecilia's inner attitude. The friend felt that Cecilia might have something to do with her dating experience, and with the fact that she was not yet married. At first Cecilia strongly resisted this suggestion, but in a series of subsequent conversations, she eventually came around to the possibility that she might have something to do with the results that she kept creating.

The back-story was that Cecilia's father was an alcoholic and was largely unavailable emotionally when Cecilia was growing up. When he was sober, her father would run the household with an iron hand. He was the dictator, and

Cecilia's mother his primary slave. The kids, as Cecilia saw them, were secondary slaves. Her father had died many years ago, but her father provided an emotionally charged model of intimate married life, and that model continued to live in Cecilia's mind.

Whenever Cecilia would get involved with a man, on the second or third date, she would find something seriously the matter with the fellow. With one man, his desire to wash her dirty dishes was perceived as a desire to control her, to tell her how she should live her life. Cecilia could not fathom the possibility that he might genuinely want to help out, knowing that Cecilia was very busy, and had not yet gotten around to washing the dishes. With another man, he wanted to hang out and talk exclusively with her at a party, instead of mingling, and that seemed unbelievably heavy-handed and controlling to Cecilia. Still another man wanted to call her every night and check-in, and this too was deemed too rigid and constraining for Cecilia.

Through several dating-related discussions with this same close friend, Cecilia opened to the possibility that these men were perhaps not quite as heavy-handed and controlling as she thought they were. To her friend, Cecelia admitted how terrified she was, terrified that she would get married and thereby become a slave, the way her mother had become a slave to her father. In light of this largely unexamined terror, it made perfect sense that Cecilia had never been married. Through these conversations, Cecilia also came to see how she was pushing men away, how she was creating barriers to intimacy, out of her fear of becoming a slave. Most importantly, Cecilia realized that as a young girl she had made an over-generalization that was still with her, and that was badly damaging her present life. Back then she had decided that marriage meant enslavement for women. She now appreciated that marriage didn't have to be that way.

Her more relaxed state, her new openness to the way she was creating in relationships with men, allowed her to have two very communicative, honest, and loving relationships with men. Each lasted a year or so, and each she ended, clearly seeing that each one of the men was not her long-term mate. Both of these relationships were entirely new experiences for Cecilia because she was able to open up to having a real-life experience of intimacy with a man, without always feeling as though the man was bossing her around, controlling her, making unreasonable demands of her, etc. While there were multiple times when that old generalization came up in relationship with these men, with her new viewpoint, she was able to quickly come back to the truth of the matter. She continues to look at what she is creating with her own consciousness, and she is now dating a new guy who realistically seems as though he could make a good long-term partner, perhaps even a husband.

Journal Questions:

(1) In what ways do you keep turning away from examining what is going on within yourself? What do you do specifically? For example, do you keep coming up with some excuse, some reason, why you are not looking at what is really going on inside you? Does this excuse, this rationalization, have any real validity?

(2) Nothing that happens in your life need ever depress you. Depression is an indication that you are stuck, that on some level you are not examining your inner state, that you are not doing the self-discovery work that life is calling you to do. There is a message behind all such experiences. To illustrate this, choose an area in your life where you feel depressed. See if you can come up with a message, a lesson that life is trying to teach you there. What is it specifically?

(3) Failures are unavoidable in life. Your failures can give you strength if you look at them with the honest and open attitude: "What is there that I have not yet learned about this situation?" Consider that if anything unpleasant happens in your life, then the roots of that experience are somewhere inside you. How could you, in some way, have contributed to a particular failure in your life, particularly a failure to bring about the change you say you that you want?

Appendix A

Related Pathwork Lectures

IF YOU WOULD like additional and more in-depth information on a particular topic addressed in a certain chapter of this book, you can read the related Pathwork lecture. These free lectures can be found at http://pathwork.org/ (click on Lectures). Alternatively, these same free lectures can be found at http://www.pathworklectures.com/ (click on All Pathwork Lectures At A Glance; the lecture you click on will then be shown in the web browser window you are then using). More powerful energy and deeper experience of the lectures is available via the unedited version of the lectures, although the reader may need to occasionally put up with a few grammatical or spelling errors when reading these unedited lectures.

Format: This Book's Chapter Number. Chapter Name – Suggested Pathwork Lecture Number – Pathwork Lecture Name

1. Asking to Know the Whole Truth – L217 – The Phenomenon of Consciousness
2. Resolving to Give Your Very Best – L196 – Commitment – Cause and Effect
3. Identifying with Your Higher Self – L14 – The Higher Self, the Lower Self, and the Mask
4. Giving Over to a Higher Purpose – L224 – Creative Emptiness
5. Dealing with Your Lower-Self Resistance – L5 – Decisions and Tests
6. Recognizing the Spiritual Meaning of Your Crisis – L183 – The Spiritual Meaning Of Crisis
7. Failing to Live Up to Your Idealized Self-Image – L83 – The Idealized Self-Image
8. Noticing How an Image Holds You Back – L38 – Images, plus L39 – Finding an Image
9. Coming Out of Denial and Going Beyond Your Mask – L14 – The Higher Self, The Lower Self, and The Mask
10. Getting That Your Thoughts Create Your Reality – L10 – Reality – Reflected Image, plus L71 – Reality and Illusion
11. Making an Inventory of Your Faults – L26 – Finding One's Faults
12. Meeting the Fear You Don't Want to Feel – L191 – Inner and Outer Experience

36. Navigating Expectations Without a Forcing Current – L71 Reality and Illusion, plus L77 – Self-Confidence

37. Discovering and Transcending Your Negative Intentionality – L195 – Identification and Intentionality: Identification with the Spiritual Self to Overcome Negative Intentionality

38. Initiating a Grounded Leap into the Unknown – L221 – Faith and Doubt in Truth or Distortion, plus L60 – The Abyss of Illusion

39. Risking the Disapproval of Others – L94 – The True Self Versus Superficial Personality Levels; Sin and Neurosis; Split Concepts Creating

40. Using Your Will Most Productively – L16 – Spiritual Nourishment

Note: All of the referenced Pathwork lectures are also available, for a charge, on a CD-ROM (go to http://www.pathwork.org/, click on Books, Music, Gifts, then on the next screen select Complete Lectures Of The Pathwork - Expanded Edition, and put it into your online shopping cart). This CD-ROM is particularly useful when searching across all the lectures for a particular word or a particular sequence of words. Some of the lectures are also now available as MP3 audio files (go to http://www.pathwork.org/, select Books, Music, Gifts, click on Download Audio Lectures, then select one of the Original Recording Lecture options, and add that to your online shopping cart). These are the original recordings delivered by Eva Broch Pierrakos, and they reach you on levels that are not just intellectual. There is a charge for each of these. Some of the lectures, read by Gary Vollbracht, are also now available for free download. These can be located by going to http://www.pathwork.org/, selecting Books, Music, Gifts, then searching for "Gary" in the search box, then adding these free lectures to your online shopping cart. These lecture recordings are great to listen to with an iPod (or similar portable music device), while driving in your car, when taking walks, or the like.

Appendix B

About the Author

CHARLES CRESSON WOOD is an empathetic and patient listener, who genuinely desires to bring meaning, significant help, and happiness, to those people who now find themselves in a stuck place, wrestling with a serious problem or a crisis. He works with deep story-telling, dream interpretation, thought experiments, role playing, and invitations to adopt a different viewpoint. These methods collectively provide a more empowered frame, a new vista about the client's situation, and from that place, previously unknown solutions emerge. He seeks truth, love, balance, self-awareness, and an objective perspective, informed by deeper guidance, a place from which previously-unappreciated strategies to problems and crises come forward. He approaches sessions with his personal coaching clients as an equal, a fellow-student of life, another imperfect human being who is stumbling along, groping for meaning and direction, and attempting to find the deeper all-encompassing-truth of life. Supporting him in this process is the profound background of the Pathwork lectures, which he has intensely studied since 1991. Charles is certified as a Pathwork "Helper," which is a type of personal psycho-spiritual counselor, a designation that takes nine years of intensive work to achieve.

Charles is also a licensed California attorney, and a management consultant specializing in computer security and privacy. He works on living a balanced life, by for example working on community-building projects, cultivating his permaculture garden, and singing call-and-response with the frogs in his pond. He has repeatedly been confronted with the perplexing situation where people don't change, even when the evidence clearly, unequivocally, and indisputably indicates that they must now change. To assist people in shifting from that painful place, he has written this book. On a similar note, Charles' other Pathwork book, entitled "Opening to Abundance" (published in 2004), guides people through a structured process where they come to know both how rich their lives genuinely are, and the great power that they have to create their heart's desire.

Charles provides coaching services in-person and remotely via the Internet. He can be reached via http://www.abundantreality.com/.

www.ingramcontent.com/pod-product-compliance
Lightning Source LLC
Chambersburg PA
CBHW070338090426
42733CB00009B/1226

* 9 780097 999144 8 *